Traveller's Joy

Traveller's Joy

Joy Everett

ATHENA PRESS
LONDON

Traveller's Joy
Copyright © Joy Everett 2007

ISBN 10-digit: 1 84748 143 4
ISBN 13-digit: 978 1 84748 143 6

First Published 2007 by
ATHENA PRESS
Queen's House, 2 Holly Road
Twickenham TW1 4EG
United Kingdom

Printed for Athena Press

Joy Everett was born in 1920 and lives in Dorset. She is married, with two children and four grandchildren. Sadly, David, the eldest, died at the age of seventeen from cystic fibrosis. Joy served with the Auxiliary Territorial Service (ATS) during the Second World War in Heavy Ack Ack, in this country and in Belgium. She was a member of The Ringwood Writers' Circle for many years. Her hobbies are reading and writing.

Contents

Too Old to Dream   15

Maria   93

Angels on a Pinhead   95

Autumn Fires   97

Fields   98

Sweet Peas   100

Peacock   102

One Life   104

Tempus Fugit   106

A Strange Romance   108

Downfall   112

Pandemic 1918–1919   114

Sunflower Fields (France)   116

Where Have All the Meadows Gone?   118

Soubes   120

Autumn Crocus   122

You Wouldn't Dare   124

Ten-Minute Walk   126

Easter Walk   128

Death of the Mountains 129

The Bombshell 131

Branston 136

Stolen Fruit 139

School Days are the Best Days! 144

Woodland Walk 148

Snowflakes and Roses 150

The Night-Wind Fairies (I) 151

Celandines 156

A Dream Visit 158

Daisies 160

Wedding Dress 161

Dead Leaves 164

January Joy 165

Kingfisher 166

The Scream (I) 167

My Bird Table 169

Single Beds 171

Blue for a Boy 173

Witch in the Cottage 179

Three Gulf War Poems 180

Year's End 184

The Red Dwarf
  (Portrait of a Chief Inspector)   186

Bluebells   188

The Night-wind Fairies (II)   190

Mum   192

Blackcurrant Jam for Our Tea   196

Not a Good Day   198

The Last Super   201

I Remember   207

Seasons   208

Man of Straw   210

The Deserted Beach   211

A Cornfield Has Two Faces   213

Lament for a Dead Twin   215

The Innocents   218

Creation versus Evolution   220

My Favourite Season   222

My Secret Place   225

My Strange Collection   227

Growing Pains   232

Christmas Reminiscences   238

Death on the High Street   242

Yesterday   245

A First Memory   250

Birdsgrove   252

Heatwave   256

Come Death, but Not Too Soon   258

WI Market   260

Stubs   262

The Miracle of Life
   (Call it Evolution or Creation)   263

The Surgery   265

The Magic of May: A Sonnet   268

Sales Talk   269

Elmo   271

Operation Bird Bath   279

Under the Belfry Tower   283

Temptation   285

Peace on Earth   290

Supermarket Shopping   292

Abortion   296

Skylarks   298

A Night-Time Garden   299

Face in the Crowd   300

Autumn Encounter   302

Missing   308

Fifty-word Mini-sagas	310
Art Form	311
Marigolds in March	312
The Art Exhibition	313
Haiku (Japanese Poetry)	315
Cowslip in a Flowerbed	316
Blue Rape	317
My Bulb Bowl	318
Ode to a Mode	319
Child of my Womb	320
Too Late	321
Haiku	322
Memories	323
The Killing Roads	324
Every Guy has His Day	326
The Apple-Dapple Lady	329
The Ghost of Sunflower Cottage	333
Worlds Apart	337
The Hitchhiker	338
Three Wishes	342
The Bid	343
Annilee – A Story of Survival	347
Sounds	351

Fading Flowers	352
An Australian Cameo	353
Voyage in a Seashell	356
Haiku	358
Imago	359
Narcissi	360
Water Lily Pond	361
The Falling of the Leaves	362
Oh Why?	363
Reflection	365
Days	367
Moonlight	369
The Meeting	373
The Double Bed	375
The One that Got Away	377
Time's Chariot	380
Surprise	381
Haiku	382
The Dangerous Skies	383
The Grass Isn't Always Greener	386
Joy is the Colour Red	390
The Voyage	392
The Scream (II)	396

The Golden Years   399

Fortune's Wheel   400

The Protest   402

Oh, To Be Young Again!   404

German Underground Hospital,
  Channel Islands   405

Butterflies   407

RIP   408

The Meet   409

Octopus   411

The Eternal Question   412

Prunus Subhirtella Autumnalis   414

Cat   415

The Reaper Cometh or
  Watch Out for Father Time   416

Dawn's Harbinger   418

Autumn Lament   420

Autumn Tapestry   421

Petunia in the Gravel   422

Ripe Fruit   423

October Rape   424

Ode to Planet Earth   426

The Last Day of the World   428

Too Old to Dream

So kiss me, my sweet
And so let us part
And when I grow too old to dream
That kiss will live in my heart.

'When I Grow Too Old to Dream', Oscar
Hammerstein and Sigmund Romberg

Chapter One

1941

Incredible as it may now seem, the only problem on my mind that day in May, almost two years into the Second World War, was that I desperately needed a new lipstick. Cities were being bombed, shipping sunk by the tonne and dreadful acts of violence perpetrated over the face of the globe, yet here was I, concerned only with the very trifling matter of a lipstick. Cosmetics were designated as luxuries at the time and their manufacture was strictly limited.

So, as I cycled home for lunch and passed a friend who informed me that the local chemist had received a delivery of cosmetics, I breathed a sigh of relief.

'Don't forget the dance this evening,' I reminded her, eager now to hurry over lunch so that I could get to the chemist before they sold out.

Our village, usually a sleepy little place, had become very lively with the arrival of various branches of the Army, which were stationed in and around the area. The twice-weekly 'hops' held in the village hall were extremely popular and we girls were always sure of plenty of partners. A hop was being held this particular evening and a glow of excitement swept over me at the thought. A restless breeze was sighing through foaming cherry trees, their petals floating down like confetti as I sped along.

Reaching home, I kicked the gate open and wheeled my bicycle down the path. The front garden was much larger than the one behind the cottage and, on this sunny spring day, it was already sprouting masses of greenery. The order had gone out to 'Dig for Victory'. Dad had obeyed to the letter. The flowerbeds, shrubs and lawns had disappeared. In their place were rows of runner been poles, early lettuce, radish, cabbage, carrots, potatoes, onions and many other vegetables as well as mounds of marrow plants and rhubarb.

Scattered all around were pots of tomato plants. Every bit of space had been utilised. It was the roses I missed most of all. When Dad dug them up, Mum had cried bitterly. The smaller back garden had suffered the same fate, but here a rambler rose, by the back door of the cottage, still clung tenaciously to the wall and was already sprouting scarlet-tipped buds.

At the end of the garden, a few hens scratched and scrambled. Every night Dad boiled up a mixture of corn and scraps for them. The smell was horrid, but we suffered it willingly, for the end result was a supply of precious eggs. These were strictly rationed in the shops, but dried egg powder was available, which was very useful. A large compost heap supplied the garden with fertiliser.

Propping my bike against the shed, I sniffed. I sniffed again. Oh no! Not savoury corned beef hash for the second time this week. I had not realised, until the war, just how many varied dishes could be concocted, using a few ounces of this commodity. The meat ration was very small so corned beef was a godsend to housewives. Even fish was in limited supply and, if Mum heard that the butcher had a delivery of rabbits in, she would hastily rush to the village to join the queue.

She had a delicious recipe for this delicacy. The joints were covered with a mixture of onion, vinegar, brown sugar, salt and mustard, and baked. Rabbit day was certainly a feast day in those hard times.

'Can't stop, Mum,' I said as dinner was dished up. 'Got to get to the chemist before they sell out of lipsticks.'

I bolted down the hash, which was not so bad if you ate it quickly. There were apple fritters for dessert; my favourite. I usually had two helpings, but today I grabbed one off the pile and munched it as I pedalled swiftly off to the village.

'A lipstick, please,' I asked, breathlessly, rushing into the chemist's shop. I was a bit frightened of the assistant, whom we nicknamed 'The Dragon', because she guarded such treasures jealously, dispensing them as though doing customers the greatest of favours.

'You've already been in and bought one this morning,' she snapped, eyeing me suspiciously, her thin lips set in a forbidding line.

I was panic-stricken. She always made me feel guilty. 'I haven't been in today, honestly,' I stammered, going red in the face. 'My existing one is finished. Please may I have one?'

I felt like going down on my knees to her, if by so doing she would agree to sell me a lipstick. I could never understand why some shopkeepers were reluctant to part with their goods when a delivery of much sought after articles arrived. I think they felt superior dispensing them, because it probably gave them a feeling of power.

'There's only one colour. No choice,' she snapped again, almost gleefully.

I could not have cared less about the colour, but in the event, it was cherry, the shade I usually wore. It was my lucky day. I then plucked up the courage to enquire if any June perfume had come in with the recent delivery.

Drawing herself up to her full height, her eyes glinting through thick, steel-rimmed spectacles, she answered sourly, 'There are more important things to worry about than tarting yourself up. You people don't seem to realise there's a war on.'

I backed out of the shop, feeling guilty yet again. I was in a reserved occupation – more of this later – but for some time had felt I ought to do more for the war effort, though I had not decided in which particular capacity I should offer my services.

Just as I reached the door, I heard a crash and realised my bicycle had fallen over; but before I could reach it, a young man in air force uniform had picked it up.

'Thanks very much,' I said as he looked the bicycle over for possible damage. Then, as he turned to assure me that it seemed all right, I found myself looking into the most gorgeous pair of dark brown eyes I had ever seen. We just stared at each other for several seconds, but before I could say any more, he walked away. I wondered who he was. Not a local lad, of that I was sure, so perhaps we now had a branch of the RAF stationed in the village.

I had no special boyfriend, but Charles, one of the local lads who was waiting for his call-up papers, was always very attentive. He was an excellent dancer and great fun to be with, but I did not want him for a regular beau. He was always trying to date me and I had to admire his persistence. I thought him rather immature, perhaps because he had never lost that little schoolboy look. Also, I did not much care for his unruly mop of red hair.

Back at the office, the dreary afternoon dragged on, only relieved by thoughts of the coming evening's pleasure. Now and again, I found myself thinking of the airman who had picked up my bike, and my heart beat a little faster when I visualised those lovely brown eyes. I hoped Mum had ironed my favourite dress. With its demure neckline, puffed sleeves and full skirt, it was really pretty, being patterned over in pink rosebuds. I need not have worried, for there it was when I got home, hanging on the line, airing. Suddenly, I experienced a violent lurch in the pit of my stomach. I had a feeling that I was about to reach an important turning point in my life.

When I was dressed, I took a final glance in the mirror. Excitement had given my cheeks a rosy glow. My grey eyes sparkled under their thick, dark brows, and my chestnut-brown hair curled softly over my temples and ears. My features, although not outstanding, were at least in proportion to my rather chubby face and my mouth was nicely shaped in a pretty Cupid's bow. I dabbed a few drops of my diminishing June perfume behind my ears and ran downstairs where my friend was waiting.

It was usually at least 8.30 p.m. before the dance really got under way, and this evening was no exception. Only a few couples were on the floor; there were not many partners, as the soldiers liked a few drinks at the nearby pub before coming to the hall. Charles was already there and we danced together a few times.

Gradually the hall began to fill. The atmosphere became warm and stuffy. Evening in Paris and Californian Poppy scent mingled with the smell of cigarette smoke and body odour (no deodorants at that time - it would be some years before they became part of one's daily toilet routine).

The MC, our milkman during the day, announced a Paul Jones. Two rings were formed, the outer composed of males, the inner of females. When the music began, both rings moved in opposite directions and, when it stopped, the girl danced with the man facing her. This sometimes resulted in a tiny girl partnering a hefty six-footer, or a tall girl dancing with someone very short, but it was all good fun and most enjoyable.

As I waltzed around, I noticed a group of RAF lads standing by the entrance. So we did have a contingent from this service in the village! As I pointed them out to my friend, when we sat down, she showed not a little interest.

A ladies' excuse-me was called. 'Come on,' my friend urged, 'let's ask the RAF to dance with us.'

Plucking up courage, I followed her to the other end of the hall. The lad nearest had his back to me. Touching him on the arm, I asked him to dance.

He spun round, a surprised expression on his face and, for the second time that day, I found myself gazing into the dark brown eyes of the airman I had met earlier. I noticed that his hair was jet black and wavy. His mouth was cute, the right bottom lip receding slightly at the corner, giving him an impish look.

A slow smile lit up his face: a frank, honest face. He recognised me and asked if my bicycle was all right, and I was able to thank him again.

The band was playing one of my favourite tunes, 'When I Grow Too Old to Dream'. Though we did not talk much, I learned his name was James, he was twenty-one and had just that week arrived in the village.

'My name is Jenny and I'm twenty,' I told him. I wanted the dance to go on and on, but all too soon, the music ended and I was back with my friend.

Much to my annoyance, Charles claimed me for the Last Waltz, although I noticed James making his way towards me. When the dance was over, Charles hung around, insisting he walk me home. I could only hope and pray that James would come to the next hop, but I went down with a feverish cold and it was nearly two weeks before I was able to go dancing again. I was frantic, worrying that he might take up with another girl or, worse still, get posted, and I would never see him again.

At last, the evening arrived when I was able to go dancing again, but there was no sign of the RAF boys when my friend and I went to the hall. My eyes continually strayed to the door and I must have been poor company for my partners. I was dancing with Charles when James came in with his friends. I noticed he was scanning the faces of the dancers and, when he saw me, he grinned broadly. I felt quite dizzy with happiness. This time he stayed by my side and we danced together all evening. Poor Charles looked so downcast and I did feel a teeny bit sorry for him.

James had written me a letter, which he had intended asking my friend to deliver had I not appeared at the dance that evening. 'Now that I've found you, I'm not letting you go,' he said. When he walked me home, he told me he was being sent away on a course for seven days, but we made a date to meet the evening of the day he was to return. I was so happy and ticked off the days on my calendar, each one seeming an eternity. I lost my appetite. I became dreamy.

At last the magic day was here. In a few hours I would be with James. I dressed carefully, choosing a pale green linen dress and matching earrings. Mum said I looked really pretty. The cherry lipstick set off the colour in my cheeks, which were pink with excitement. My eyes were starry.

James was waiting at the top of the lane; he took my hand in his and we walked across the fields. I shall never forget that evening. Buttercups glowed more brightly than I ever remembered and May and Elder blossom scented the soft evening air with a cloying fragrance. From nearby woods, a cuckoo called, and a pair of courting doves cooed incessantly from a tall tree.

We sat on an old log and James put an arm around me. 'When I volunteered for the RAF, I asked for air crew,' he explained, 'but they were full at the time. I'm afraid my posting came through while I was away and I commence training in a week's time.'

My heart sank. Not only was he going away but also his work would be dangerous. I had read about bomber crew losses. They were terrible. I was distraught.

'What exactly will your work be?' I asked him in a small voice. When he told me he would be training to become a wireless operator/air gunner, I thought, Oh my God. The tail-end Charlie often had the worst of it.

Then he drew me to him and held me close. 'I want you to be my girl, Jenny. Please say yes.'

I hesitated. I wanted a permanent boyfriend, but one with his feet on the ground, who at least had some chance of survival, not someone in such a dangerous occupation. But when I looked into those deep brown eyes, I knew I was so very much in love that whatever job he did, it would be all right with me.

'Yes, James, I'll be your girl,' I answered.

He gave me his first kiss, a sweet, tender kiss. And then we kissed again, long and lingering.

'I've something for you,' he said, taking a small box from his pocket. 'I was able to get home for a few hours while on the course, so I collected this. I hope you like it. Please will you wear it always?'

Opening the box, I saw, against a background of faded red velvet, a lovely eternity ring. 'I can't accept this, James,' I remonstrated. But, taking it from the box, he placed it on my engagement finger. 'It belonged to my great-grandmother,' he told me. 'Later on, I'll give you a proper engagement ring, darling. You belong to me now.'

Happiness made me speechless and we just sat there on that log for ages, hugging each other.

We spent an unforgettable week, but all too soon it was time for him to leave and I saw him board the train through tear-filled eyes.

Chapter Two

1942–1943

Luckily, the first part of James's training did not take him too far away and we would be together whenever he could get a pass, either at his home or mine. How precious were those hours; how quickly they passed! But, as time went on, and he was posted further away, visits were less frequent.

Then, one day, he came to see me, a fully-fledged sergeant wireless operator/air gunner. I was so proud of him but terribly fearful.

'I'll be OK, darling,' he reassured me. 'You mustn't worry. It isn't as bad as you imagine.'

But, of course, I fretted about him and, one day, when he came unexpectedly on a short leave and told me he'd been on a one-thousand bomber raid over Bremen the previous night, I realised I had to take a more active part in the war effort. My only contribution so far was a few hours a week doing Red Cross work. My office job with a clothing company, evacuated from London for the safer haven of our village, was considered a reserved occupation, but an older person exempt from military service could quite well have been employed to do it – and it was not very interesting anyway. I now requested my firm to release me for National Service.

It was some time before I received a summons from the War Office, requesting, nay, ordering, that I present myself at a Women's Auxiliary Territorial Service (ATS) training camp. It seemed that failure to comply with this notification would result in dire consequences as far as I was concerned.

James managed to get away for a couple of days. He had been promoted to flight sergeant and said he would apply for a commission. 'I'll be able to put a bit more away so that, when the war is over, we can buy a home of our own. You will save yourself for me, darling?' he said, holding me in his arms.

'You know I will, James,' I promised. 'I'll never love anyone else, never.'

On the day I was to report to training camp, Mum accompanied me to London and saw me off on the train that would take me to my destination. I had never been away from home before and shed a few tears on the journey.

That first week was a nightmare. We never seemed to have time to draw breath. Instead of Dad waking me up gently with a steaming hot cup of tea, we were roused at some unearthly hour by our corporal, who screamed at the top of her voice as she rushed down the hut, thumping each of us on our backsides. Then it was a mad dash to barrack beds and to get to breakfast before all the food was consumed. At first, I thought it was very bad manners to see how everyone grabbed the toast and bread and butter, but before long, I was guilty of doing the same. It was that or go without, and one did not dare do as Oliver did where the cooks were concerned.

The day after we arrived, we were taken to the stores and issued with a kitbag, which was gradually filled to overflowing with items necessary to clothe us as fully-fledged members of the ATS. I could not see how all that stuff was ever going to be packed tidily into that kitbag, for as we trudged round, we were in danger of leaving trails of clothing in our wake. We staggered under bundles of khaki bloomers, blouses and bras. We were even issued with a hussif, which contained mending materials. All these garments, as well as various other odds and ends we were issued with, had to be marked with our name and number. A tedious task performed when the day's activities were over.

One afternoon our corporal came into the hut carrying a large pile of brown paper and told us we must parcel up our civilian clothes to be sent home. It was an awful moment when they were handed in for posting. 'Goodbye, Civvy Street,' one of the girls said, sadly.

Our days were filled with drill sessions, lectures, fatigues, medicals and inoculations. I found it very embarrassing having to dress and undress in front of other people, and extremely tiresome having to store my belongings in a small cupboard. Little did I realise that later, when posted to other units, our only form of storage would be a soldier's box measuring about thirty inches long by twenty inches high.

I was thoroughly miserable at first until James wrote to say he was coming to see me. How he managed the long journey from his base, I never knew. He had been on ops the night before and looked so tired. There were shadows under his eyes. Oh, how happy I was to see him waiting at the camp gate and I flew into his arms. It was bliss to be with him, if only for a few hours, and after that everything seemed so much better. I even began to enjoy the endless drilling and got used to living in the company of so many females. There was always someone ready with a joke and a helping hand.

It took us some time to get used to saluting officers and, one afternoon, I and a couple of the girls I had become friendly with were in the town, when we were berated by an irate ATS officer for failing to give her the necessary salute. After that we saluted anyone we thought might be entitled, even making the ghastly mistake of smartly saluting a much uniformed male cinema attendant, much to his surprise and obvious delight.

Soon it was time for my first leave and how good it was to get into civvy clothes again. James also had some leave and we spent many happy hours taking long walks and cycle rides, listening to our favourite records, or going up to town to see a show.

We discussed plans for getting married. James said that when he put the wedding ring on my finger he would be promising to take care of me for the rest of my life. 'I can't make that promise yet, darling,' he explained, 'because I've got lots more ops to get through, but when I complete my second tour and if the war news is encouraging, we'll think about setting a date.'

I would like to have married James as soon as possible and told him I was prepared to risk anything, but he was so afraid he would suffer some sort of dreadful injury which might leave him permanently disabled. It just wouldn't be fair, he argued, and if we married and I had a child, there was the possibility he might be killed and I would be left to struggle on alone.

He gave me a beautiful engagement ring, but I decided to keep the eternity ring on my engagement finger, leaving the new ring at home. I had a strange feeling that if I continued to wear the first ring he gave me, it would act as a lucky charm so I never took it off.

But, all too quickly the hours passed and I was kissing him goodbye and on my way back to training camp.

Chapter Three

1943

I had hoped I might be fortunate and get a posting not too far from James, but it was not to be. I was sent to a Royal Artillery Training HQ miles away from his base, where I was now to join a mixed, Heavy Ack Ack regiment to train as a telephonist.

James was now in Cornwall, attached to Coastal Command, and our paths were destined not to cross for some time, although letters were a great consolation.

On arrival at my new posting, yet more clothing was issued. This consisted of slacks, battledress tops, leather jerkins, thick grey socks, boots, gaiters and tin helmets. Oh, how we suffered in those boots until we wore them in! Oh, those painful blisters!

I had thought my spell at training camp had hardened me to the rigours of army life, but I was to have a rude awakening. Not only did we attend classes and lectures applicable to our trade, but it seemed that the most important part of the course was to learn to drill according to the stringent standards set by the Royal Artillery.

Our drill instructor, a little cockney sergeant major, beady eyed, sharp nosed and small of tooth, put me in mind of an animated ferret. However, when he shouted, his voice reverberated right across the parade ground. It was quite remarkable that someone so small possessed such efficient vocal cords.

'Right, get fell in there, youse lot,' he screamed, when we assembled for our first drill session. Now, this particular parade ground was swept by the four winds of heaven and, in the month of February, they were at their worst, blasting us from all angles. We prayed he would not keep us too long. The Navy, Army and Air Force Institutes (NAAFI) canteen beckoned with its mugs of hot, strong tea, and sticky buns, but our instructor was in his element with a bunch of rookies and so he made the most of it.

After putting us through our paces for a while, he called us to a halt, then stood us at ease.

'Never 'ave I seen a mob like youse lot,' he bellowed. 'Didn't they teach you nothink at youse last depot? Youse is just a rabble, that's what youse is, a rabble. 'Ow dare youse defame this 'allowed ground. And youse there,' pointing his cane at one of the girls, 'youse is a disgrace. Come out 'ere.'

The unfortunate culprit was then marched up and down and, to make matters worse, several interested spectators had gathered on the edge of the parade ground. However hard she tried, she just could not get the sequence of arms and legs right. The more the instructor shouted at her, the more agitated she became, eventually bursting into tears. This was too much for him and out came a further torrent of vituperation, at the end of which he paused, then yelled, "Ow dares youse blub on my parade ground. Get orf and go back to youse barrack room, and if others of youse feels like blubbing, you can get orf too.'

How we dreaded those sessions, but somehow we all got through our training and even managed to give a fair performance when the Regiment finally assembled for the passing out parade, before we marched through the town to the railway station en route for firing camp. We were led by the Royal Artillery Band – all very stirring. We were proud to belong to that branch of the service.

There had, of course, been various rumours as to our destination, but the Army never saw fit to take us into their confidence. I learnt later that the most reliable source when a move was imminent was the cookhouse. How they ever obtained the information I never found out, but they invariably got it right.

Our destination was in fact the Isle of Anglesey. Here the Regiment underwent further training. The gunners practised their firing skills by shooting at a large red sleeve, which was towed behind an aircraft flying over the sea. I thought these pilots had a terrifying job, knowing that the firing was coming from a lot of greenhorns, but, as far as I can remember, there were no casualties, at least while our Regiment was there.

The telephonists now joined with the spotters and became proficient at recognising every type of aircraft from all angles, both allied and enemy. As well as attending lectures, we did our share of fatigues, peeling pounds of potatoes, washing up greasy pans and preparing hundreds of slices of bread and butter. We also took turns in keeping the camp tidy and the ablutions clean.

Every day an ATS sergeant took us for PT on the beach. March on the Isle of Anglesey is not to be recommended for this type of activity, especially when you are clad only in thin shorts and tops. We froze! As soon as we were dismissed, there would be a mad rush to the NAAFI for a reviver – a piping hot mug of tea and, if we were lucky, a nice gooey jam doughnut.

At the end of our training, we were granted seven days' leave and told to report back to a gun site near Liverpool.

James was still flying down in Cornwall and there was no chance of our meeting, though I did stay with his parents for a few days – but I was so lonely without him there.

While I was home, Charles came to see me. He was now in the RAF, attached to a Rescue and Recovery unit. I just could not see him dealing with crashed aircraft and dead bodies and shivered when he related some of his experiences. 'Please, don't tell me any more,' I begged him, and he was very contrite.

'Sorry, old girl,' he said. 'How thoughtless of me. Gee, that boy of yours sure is a lucky chap. I wish I was in his shoes.'

He asked me to write to him now and again. I hesitated, but he looked so dejected that I had not the heart to refuse. When I agreed, his face lit up. 'You know I'll always be around if you want me at any time, Jenny.'

'You really are a dear, Charles,' I answered, giving him a brief kiss on the cheek, but it was to be a very long time before we met again.

Soon after returning to my unit, I was promoted to Lance Corporal, which gave me a bit more to do. The roster for the telephonists was difficult to work out, as the command post had to be manned by two of us throughout the day and night. Leave, twenty-four hour passes and sickness had to be taken into account and I also tried to give the girls as much variation as possible in their shifts, besides ensuring that they had their fair share of opportunities to attend dances held in the camp and to accept invitations from other units in the area. My pay rise was useful, enabling me to send a small amount home occasionally, which Mum put into my post office savings account for me.

German raids were now non-existent in our part of the country, and much of our time was spent in exercises called 'Bullseyes' to make sure we were at readiness if our area came under attack again.

Mail, usually distributed in the NAAFI at morning break, was one of the high spots of our day. One morning, I received several letters, including one from James. Tearing it open eagerly, I read that he had some leave due. He wanted me to try and get a seventy-two hour pass so that we could make arrangements to get married. I had thought he would wait until he had completed his second tour and was on a rest period, but he told me that he was two thirds of the way through his present tour and wanted to set a date for a June wedding to coincide with the end of his present tour. He was flying from a base in Yorkshire.

In great excitement, I rushed up to battery office to put in a request for a pass. Several days went by and I was in a turmoil of anxiety, but leave was finally granted. Within a few days, I was on my way home.

Those three days passed so quickly. There was so much to do in preparation for the wedding. Coupons were required for the purchase of clothing and materials – service personnel were only issued with a few of these on a yearly basis, but a dressmaker in the village unearthed a lovely piece of white silk. We discussed the style of dress she was to make; a princess line with full skirt, heart-shaped neck, and long sleeves tapering to a point over the wrists. With it, I would wear a short veil and a headband of real pink rosebuds. We chose the wedding ring and arranged a date for mid-June.

'It won't be long now, darling,' James murmured, holding me close when the time came for us to part. 'Soon you'll be my wife and when this war is over, we'll settle down and be happy ever after.' He kissed me and, as he did so, a cold blast of wind swept through my body.

'Please take care, dearest, and remember I shall love you forever,' I whispered. Then the train drew out of the station and I lost sight of him.

Nothing was going to happen to James, I told myself. He was a survivor. Quite soon we would be married and, when the war was over, we would buy a little home and be together for the rest of our lives. There would be no more heartache and partings.

Chapter Four

A week before my leave, Mum had written to say she had collected my wedding dress. 'It's lovely,' she wrote. 'The dressmaker has sewn a little blue bow in one of the seams and finished off the hem with a hair from her head, for luck.'

I did not think it was possible for anyone to be so happy and the night before I was due home, I was so excited I barely slept a wink.

Returning from an early breakfast, I saw that the girls were still in various stages of rising. Oh well, I thought, it isn't my responsibility today if they're late and miss breakfast.

As I picked up my haversack prior to leaving, various remarks of a very suggestive nature were flung at my retreating back, but I grinned good-naturedly and, with a wave of my hand, hurried off to catch the train which would take me to London, where I was to meet James.

We were to spend our honeymoon in a little cottage in Worcestershire, which a relation of James's had lent us. I could not believe I was going to have him all to myself in our own little place for a few precious days. 'Only one more op to go, darling,' he had written in his last letter. 'They usually give you an easy one, so don't worry.'

As I made my way to the station, my step was light. I felt carefree and seemed to be walking on air. A delivery of make-up had arrived at the NAAFI a few days previously and I wafted along in an aura of June perfume.

We had arranged to meet at King's Cross station. There were already several people waiting at the barrier, but I walked round for a while to kill time. As I passed the buffet, the strains of our special tune floated through the open door, the melody we had first danced to – 'When I Grow Too Old to Dream', and I pictured James holding me close. An elderly porter shuffled towards me. I enquired if the York train would be in on time, but he was obviously tired of being bothered with this sort of question and informed me in a grumpy voice that it was always late and might not run at all. 'There's a war on, you know,' he added for good measure.

Not even this pessimistic reply could dampen my spirits. Of course the train would run, it just had to, I reassured myself. Tomorrow was my wedding day and my bridegroom was on that train. Nothing was going to go wrong to upset our plans.

A murmur went up from the crowd which had now clustered round the barrier, as a porter scribbled in white chalk on a piece of board: 'York train arriving in five minutes'.

I took up my position by the bookshop, our planned rendezvous. The minutes dragged by, each an eternity, and still the track stretching away in the distance remained obstinately empty.

'Here it comes,' someone called, excitedly.

My throat tightened. A thrill of anticipation set every nerve in my body tingling. My hands were trembling as the train snorted, hissed and spluttered into the station. Doors were flung open and a seething mass of khaki, navy and air force blue spewed onto the platform, then surged towards the barrier.

Standing on tiptoe and craning my neck, I eagerly searched the faces in the oncoming crowd. All around me, people were kissing, laughing, crying and hugging each other. I was almost swept off my feet. Hundreds of faces in the crowd, all anonymous, all featureless, except one as far as I was concerned. One special face.

Then I realised the platform was deserted. The crowd had dispersed. I alone remained and, as the barrier clanged shut, the train, its doors hanging open and now denuded of its human cargo, resembled the backbone of a skeleton. Someone had rubbed the writing off the board.

I stood motionless for a long time, my excitement rapidly evaporating as a terrible sensation of numbness engulfed me. Waves of bitter disappointment swept over me.

Gradually I roused myself and slowly walked away, my feet dragging like lumps of lead. The day, which had dawned sunny and blue-skied, was now overcast. Black clouds had gathered and a light drizzle began to fall.

My steps took me into a little teashop not far from the station and I ordered a pot of tea. The hot liquid gradually revived me and I began to think more clearly. How stupid I'd been, I told myself. Of course there was a perfectly good explanation to account for James's non-appearance. He'd missed the train, the connection, or the transport from his base had broken down. There'd be a message waiting for me when I reached home.

As I got up to leave, I heard the BBC news being broadcast. The announcer reported that a large force of RAF planes of Bomber Command had carried out attacks on industrial targets in the Ruhr the previous night. 'Twelve of our aircraft failed to return,' he added.

An ice-cold hand seemed to clutch at my heart. I sat down again, feeling faint, as I felt myself being sucked down into an abyss of hopeless despair. James was on that raid, of that I was sure. 'Please, God,' I prayed, 'let James be safe. Let him come back to me.'

'You all right, dearie?' a waitress asked. 'You look terrible.'

'Yes, don't worry,' I answered shakily. 'I just came over a bit dizzy.'

'Well, you sit there for a bit and I'll bring you some more tea,' she said, kindly.

'No! No! I must be going but thank you very much.' And I made my way into the street.

What was I to do? Go straight home? Or ought I to go and see James's parents? I decided on the latter course and, within an hour, I was knocking on their door.

'Whatever is the matter, dear?' his mother asked, an astonished look on her face. 'I thought you were both going to your home. Where is James? Why isn't he with you?'

'He didn't come on the York train. Did you hear the BBC News earlier? I listened in a teashop. There was a big raid last night and twelve of our planes failed to return. Surely James wasn't on that raid. You would have heard by now if he was posted missing, wouldn't you?' My words came tumbling out so fast that I was quite breathless when I had finished speaking.

'Now come and sit down,' his mother insisted, 'and calm yourself. We haven't heard anything yet. I hardly think James was on that raid. He probably missed the train.'

But as time went on, it was decided his father should go and have a word with the local vicar. Perhaps he would put a call through to James's base and find out what had happened. He could also explain that we were getting married the next day and arrangements would have to be cancelled if the news was bad.

I do not know how we got through the next hour and, when eventually James's dad came cycling down the road, we both flew to the door. But one look at his face told us the worst. 'He's missing. James is missing. He didn't return from that raid last night,' he said, brokenly.

I suppose shock affects people in different ways. I could not cry. My stomach tightened into a hard knot. I felt as though a bucket of ice-cold water had been thrown over me. From feeling on top of the world only that morning, I was now at rock bottom.

How could I face my parents? They would be heartbroken, but I wanted to stay with James's parents in case any news came through, though the only communication they received was the expected telegram regretting that James was missing, followed by a letter from his squadron leader to the effect that

James's plane had been with the squadron on the return journey over the Zuyder Zee.

I would not let myself believe that James had been killed. He would be a prisoner of war and come back to me when the war was over. Perhaps he was even now making his escape through Holland, being passed along by the Underground movement and eventually find his way back to this country. No, I would never give up waiting for him and praying that, one day, we would be together again.

My leave at an end, I sadly packed my belongings, having already written to my particular friend, giving her the news. She would tell the girls why I had not got married. I did not want to do any explaining but, even so, I dreaded facing them. When I entered the hut, I gave them no chance to commiserate. 'Don't say anything, please,' I implored. I changed into my battledress, telling them that I would be in the Command Post if anyone wanted me.

Weeks passed with no news of James and then, one day, I received a letter from his mother saying she had been informed by the Air Ministry that, except for James, the bodies of the rest of his crew had been found, washed up off the Dutch coast near Den Helder. They regretted that James must be presumed dead. I would not believe it. Somehow, with every fibre of my being, I knew he was still alive. I would never accept the fact that he had been killed on that fateful night, at least not until more definite news was received that his body had actually been found.

I tried to keep busy and put my name down for as many duties as possible. I functioned like an automaton. The girls tried in vain to make dates for me with several of the gunners, and tried to persuade me to go to dances with them outside the camp, but I would have none of it. However, I was glad of their comradeship. It was impossible to be unhappy all the time and many an evening was spent talking of our experiences, happy, sad, or hilarious. There was Connie, a cockney, who amused us many times with a tale of how she came to be put on a charge because she lost a boot and so had thrown its mate into a dustbin.

Unfortunately for her, someone retrieved it and reported the matter. She spiced the story with her usual brand of expletives and, by the time she came to the end, we would be shaking with laughter.

Then there was Elsie, somewhat fey, who was convinced she was a clairvoyant; she was always keen to read our palms or the tea leaves. Sometimes she would go off into a deep trance and have to lie down, much to everyone's amusement. We were sure she was putting on an act.

The months passed and still there was no news of James, but I went on cherishing the hope that he was alive and would come back to me one day.

Chapter Five

1944

The Second Front was now well under way and the powers that be decided to send a mixed, Heavy Ack Ack Regiment overseas. Volunteers were required to make up gaps in the chosen Regiment – girls were not sent overseas against their wishes. Also, some were considered medically unfit, or had to stay in this country on compassionate grounds.

Although we had been well trained, we had never put the training into operation against the enemy and, for a long time, I had nurtured a hope that I might be on duty when our guns smashed a Jerry plane out of the sky in revenge for James. So I put my name down on the list of volunteers and within a few days was posted to the Regiment being sent overseas.

On arrival at my new camp, yet more kit was issued. This included long johns, sheepskin gloves and fur jackets. Rumours were rife. We were being sent to Russia, to Iceland, or even to Norway. It was all speculation.

We were soon to find out for, one very frosty morning before dawn, we were put on a train which took us to Portsmouth and the following day we boarded ship. As we moved off, a few dockworkers waved and cheered and the haunting strains of

Handel's Largo floated across the water. Where it came from, we had no idea, but I never hear that piece of music without thinking back to that grey morning in November 1944.

The night was spent in the waters off Beachy Head, sleeping in our clothes over which we wore life jackets. Going on deck the next morning, we saw that we were in the middle of a huge convoy. It was a magnificent sight. As far as the eye could see, ships of all shapes and sizes rode at anchor.

That morning, we arrived at Ostend where we stayed a few days; then a long journey in trucks took all the Batteries to their final destinations. Ours was out in the country, about ten kilometres from Brussels.

Facilities on the gun site were extremely primitive; it had been constructed very hurriedly after the site we were to have occupied was destroyed by flying bombs. The ablutions were awful. Strips of sacking hung at the entrance to each toilet, which consisted of a bucket. To save embarrassment when enthroned, one resorted either to whistling, humming or singing, thus indicating that the cubicle was occupied. Tin washbowls were in short supply and hot water available only once a day; there was never enough of that either. No baths had been installed, but we were taken once a week by truck to a nearby town so that we could use the public baths.

The winter of 1944–1945 was bitterly cold: thick frosts and deep snow. We certainly realised why we had been issued with all that warm clothing. The stove, which stood in the middle of each hut, was only lit in the evening, when we would huddle round it in spite of the obnoxious fumes it gave off. Many a foray was made after dark to raid the coke heap for extra supplies of fuel. We became very crafty at this; fortunately, we were never caught, though we had some narrow escapes.

Flying bombs – we called them 'Divers' – droned over all that first night and we were eager to get fully operational so that we could have a go at them.

As time went on, the Regiment saw plenty of action and accounted for the destruction of many Divers, as well as some German planes.

I was now a tele-spotter; our duties in the Command Post consisted of marking plots on a large map according to data relayed from headquarters; taking down weather reports and other information; as well as manning the Telescope Identificator, which stood outside on the gun park. The latter activity was done in pairs, one searching bearing 00–1800 and the other bearing 1800–3600. This instrument was manned throughout the whole twenty-four hours.

After sounding the alert one night, we tracked a large black shape flying in and out of the clouds, on the Identificator; we identified it as a Junker 88. The Height Finder and Predictor girls were on target; the Radar girls had it on their screen.

'On bearing, on angle, on range approaching,' someone shouted. This was followed by the order from the Gun Position Officer, 'All guns fire.' The noise was, as usual, deafening. After a few bursts, the plane suffered a direct hit, exploded and spiralled earthwards. Then came the order, 'All guns cease firing – target destroyed.' A tremendous cheer echoed around the Gun Park, but I found I could not join in.

I felt sick inside, thinking only that somewhere out there, someone's husband, brother, son or fiancé lay dead, probably burnt beyond recognition. I had thought revenge would be sweet. I realised I was wrong.

The Ardennes debacle caused great consternation. As each day passed, plots on our map showed the enemy gaining ground and advancing in the direction of Liège, not too many miles from our site. Plans were put into operation for all ATS personnel to be evacuated, if necessary, by the Royal Army Service Corps. Thankfully the Germans were driven back, though not without great loss to the Allies.

The war was going well, but one great obstacle remained. The Rhine had yet to be crossed; this took place in March 1945. The day before this event, a notice was put up outside battery office from Field Marshall Montgomery, headed 'Personal Message from the C-in-C'. These are a few lines from this message:

> 21 Army Group will now cross the Rhine. Over the Rhine, then, let us go and good hunting to all on the other side. May 'the Lord mighty in battle' give us the victory in this our latest undertaking, as He has done in all our battles since we landed in Normandy on D-Day.

The following morning we were informed that a large formation of allied aircraft was heading in our direction. As it passed over the gun site, we gazed incredulously, as wave after wave of planes towing gliders flew over very low in what seemed to be a never-ending stream. We waved both arms, the girls blew kisses and everyone shouted, 'Good luck, boys, God bless.' There was a strange silence after they had disappeared. How many of those lads would make the return journey? we wondered.

In May 1945, the war was over. I strolled down to the Battery Office to read the official bulletin. The scrap of paper fluttered feebly from the noticeboard. I thought of all that lay behind those few words: the heartache, pain, torture, deprivation, tears, courage and sacrifice. People would celebrate victory. There would be great rejoicing, but to me, it seemed almost sacrilege, like dancing on millions of graves. I thought of James. If he had survived – and I sometimes had a strange feeling that he was indeed alive somewhere – we would be making plans to settle down in our own home. What was I going to do with my life now? A great sadness swept over me and I turned away, my eyes full of tears.

Passing the NAAFI, I heard sounds of celebration. Drying my eyes, I joined in and, for the first time in my life, got rather drunk.

We were very sad when the Regiment was disbanded and we were posted to other units, either in the UK or Belgium. I was sent to Brussels, where I worked in GHQ Second Echelon for a further period until my release.

Chapter Six

1946–1956

In June 1946 I was demobbed and, as I made the journey home, I thought about the last few years. It would be strange to be a civilian again, free to do whatever I chose, not answerable to Army authority. I knew I would miss the companionship I had enjoyed while in the services. Suddenly, I felt very alone now that I was no longer under their jurisdiction and I realised it was not going to be easy to readjust.

As the train drew into the station of my hometown, I looked for Dad, who always came to meet me, but, to my surprise, he was not there, though Charles was waiting by the barrier.

'Heard you were coming home today,' he said, his face wreathed in smiles. 'So thought I'd come along and help with your kit. Got the old man's car outside. Hop in.'

I felt quite surprised that I was pleased to see him. He had certainly matured. His face had thinned down. He was more confident and that little schoolboy look had vanished. Even his mop of red hair had been tamed, but his grey-green eyes still flashed with a mischievous twinkle.

'I'm being demobbed soon,' he told me, piling my luggage into the car. 'You'll want to be with your parents this evening, but how about a run out in the country tomorrow? I'm sure Dad will lend me the car again if there's enough petrol. We'll celebrate our demobs.'

'That would be rather fun, Charles,' I answered. 'Call for me about seven o' clock tomorrow evening.'

Later, as I went through my wardrobe for something suitable to wear, I found the green linen dress I had worn the evening James had given me the eternity ring. I resolutely folded it up and put it away at the back of the drawer. I still, of course, wore the ring, feeling that doing so might act as a charm and bring James back to me.

Eventually I chose a sleeveless blue dress and a matching bow for my hair. The following evening, as Charles handed me into the car, he said I looked lovely. His words sent a small thrill running through me. Suddenly, it felt good to be with him.

'I'm getting my old job back with good prospects of promotion,' he told me. 'What are your plans, Jenny?'

'Oh, I'll try for a job in London and, later, I want to buy a flat of my own,' I answered.

We had now drawn up outside a little thatched pub. The interior was charming, dimly lit by small red lamps in spite of the hour. Bowls of scarlet roses stood on low tables. I began to relax. Charles was very attentive and regaled me with lots of funny stories about his experiences in the RAF. After a couple of drinks, I felt a bit light-headed. The owner found out that I had just been demobbed after serving overseas and insisted on buying us more drinks.

'Let's get some fresh air, Charles,' I suggested. 'It's so hot in here!'

Outside, a honeysuckle bush scented the balmy June air. Charles broke off a twig and stuck it through the bow in my hair.

After driving a couple of miles, he stopped the car in a country lane and we climbed a wooden gate into a field.

'Come on, Charles, race you to that hayrick,' I called, running through the long grass. Reaching it, we collapsed breathless in a heap of straw. Above us, a new moon seemed to be swaying to and fro, to and fro, and millions of stars flashed and shimmered.

'Look at the moon, Charles,' I began, but further words were stopped by his passionate kisses. His hands caressed my body. I responded to his ardour and, under that swaying, silver crescent moon, our twin girls were conceived.

I slept late the following morning and, as memory of the previous evening flooded in, I stretched luxuriously. Charles would be on his way back to his base in Scotland, but had promised to let me know the date of his demob. Then it came to me that this was the first time for many months that I had not thought of James immediately on waking.

'You know I've always loved you, Jenny,' Charles had whispered as he kissed me goodnight.

A knock on the front door interrupted my reverie and, glancing out of the window, I saw a florist's van parked in the road outside our cottage. Putting on my slippers and dressing gown, I ran downstairs to find Mum holding a large bouquet of deep-red roses.

'They're for you, Jenny. Here's a card,' and she held it out to me.

'Darling Jenny,' I read. 'Please marry me. I love you so much.' It was signed 'Charles'.

I was staggered at his suggestion. Marrying him was certainly not on my list of priorities. He was rather a sweetie though and I did not want to hurt his feelings. It would be nice to have him as an occasional escort, but I had plans of my own.

However, I was soon to find out that one's plans do not always work out as one expects, for a week before Charles was demobbed, I realised I was pregnant.

'We'll get married as soon as possible, Jenny darling,' Charles exclaimed when I gave him the news. 'I promise I'll make you very happy.'

So our wedding was arranged to take place a month later. It was to be quiet, although Charles would have liked all the trimmings. I chose a cream linen suit for the ceremony, with a saucy little hat to match, and Charles ordered a small posy of scarlet rosebuds for me to carry.

If my thoughts, at times, strayed to James – which they quite often did – I would hastily push them to the back of my mind. I was soon to start a new life as Charles's wife. James was dead; he must be. I had to accept that fact. Now I must devote my life to Charles and our child.

But the night before I was to be married, I had a disturbing dream. I dreamt I was in church, walking down the aisle, but the bridegroom waiting at the chancel steps was not Charles. The figure standing there staring at me was James, my James. With a great cry of joy, I let go of my father's arm, threw my posy into the congregation and ran headlong towards him.

But, no matter how swiftly I ran, I could not reach him. I seemed to be on a treadmill, getting nowhere. Then I was aware that, although he was staring at me, there was a faraway look in his eyes and, with a gasp of dismay, I saw that he had not recognised me. In desperation, I screamed at the top of my voice, 'James, James, it's me, Jenny!'

The dream faded and, when I awoke, the sun was streaming through my bedroom window and Dad was there with my breakfast tray. On it was a deep-red rose attached to a parcel wrapped in tissue.

'Charles called earlier and left this for you,' he said.

Inside the parcel, nestling in a box lined with cream velvet, lay a two-strand necklace of beautiful pearls. A card tucked inside read: 'For the loveliest girl in the world from the luckiest guy in the world. Wear these today, darling.'

Later, walking down the aisle, no ghosts lurked in the shadows as Charles, with tears of happiness in his eyes, came forward to take my hand in his.

Our honeymoon was spent in the Lake District in a small hotel on the shores of a large lake. The setting was idyllic. Charles insisted I had breakfast in bed every morning, in spite of my protests. 'I'm not ill, Charles,' I would remind him. 'I'm only having a baby.'

The weather was wonderful and under Charles's care I blossomed. I felt I had emerged from a dark valley into the sunlight.

But, being married to Charles did not mean I had forgotten James. He was always there at the back of my mind – how could it be otherwise?

Just before our marriage, a cottage owned by Charles's father had become vacant and we were able to move in on our return. It was very spacious, the roof thatched, the windows mullioned; I fell in love with it right away. I planned to plant a rose garden in the front so we decided to call it 'Rose Cottage'. It had been much neglected in the war years and we had great fun putting it to rights. Furniture and linen were still rationed, being manufactured to wartime utility standards, but relatives and friends were helpful, turning out attics and cupboards for useful items.

Although, as time passed, we gradually refurnished as goods became more freely available, I often looked back nostalgically to the days when we had to make do with odd pieces of furniture, crockery that did not match and different patterned curtains at all the windows. The cottage had a certain charm then which no amount of modern hangings and fitments could match.

I was now seven months' pregnant and becoming plumper by the day, much to the fond amusement of Charles. I mentioned my weight when I went for my next check-up and, after my doctor had examined me, he told me to prepare myself for a shock. 'You're having twins, Jenny,' he said.

When I gave Charles the news, his face was a picture.

'What a clever couple we are, darling. Now you'll have to give in and get help in the house.'

I had been against this when he had mentioned it earlier, but now felt it might be sensible, so when I next saw our postman, Bob Ridger, who had lived in the village all his life, I asked him if he knew of anyone suitable.

'As a matter of fact,' he said, 'now that our three are married and living away, my wife is thinking about doing a few hours a week. Would you like me to send her round?'

As soon as I saw her coming up the drive, I felt sure she would do. Amy Ridger was a typical countrywoman, round faced, red cheeked and put one in mind of a Cox's orange pippin. Her hair, coiled in a neat bun, was silver grey. She wore a brown suit and this, coupled with a pair of soft, brown eyes, gave her the look of a small furry animal.

Amy Ridger preferred to be called by her surname so Ridger she was always called. I engaged her there and then and never regretted it. She was an absolute treasure, as well as being an adept cook and needlewoman. Bob, her husband, came in twice a week to help in the garden so, all in all, it was a very satisfactory arrangement. As the weeks went by, I wondered how I would have coped without them.

I now had only a couple of weeks to go before the twins were due and, after dining with friends one evening, we arrived home rather late. We had only been in bed a short while when I experienced a sharp pain in the middle of my back. I turned over in an effort to get more comfortable, but the pain persisted. I realised I had commenced labour.

'Charles! Charles!' I began, digging him in the ribs. 'I think the babies have started. Wake up!'

'What! What!' he mumbled sleepily.

'It's the babies,' I shouted.

Leaping out of bed, half asleep, he grabbed his clothes. First he tried to put both feet in one trouser leg, then put his shoes on the wrong feet. Finally, he tripped over the sheepskin rug and went flying across the floor.

I sat up in bed, shaking with laughter, in spite of my niggling pain. 'Simmer down, Charles. The babies won't be born for hours,' I told him. But secretly I was not so sure; I was relieved when we arrived at the nursing home.

Things happened very quickly after that and by 5 a.m. our twin girls were born, both with masses of flaming red hair.

In the weeks that followed my confinement, I did indeed find that we had an absolute treasure in Ridger. She lived with us for several weeks so that she could help with the feeding. I was able to breastfeed, supplementing with bottles, and here she proved invaluable. Sleeping in an adjoining room, she would be out of bed at the slightest sound and bring the babies to me, then make up the bottles. Charles was a great help in winding and changing and, between us, we happily weathered those first few months.

The twins thrived, keeping us busy, and with various village commitments, I found life very full. Sometimes, on waking, my thoughts turned to James and I would experience a terrible sharp pang of sadness but, as the day's activities claimed my attention, these thoughts would recede to the inner recesses of my mind.

It so happened that one Saturday afternoon I was at a loose end. Charles was tinkering with the car, Ridger was making cakes and the twins were helping Bob Ridger in the garden. They were his willing slaves and, glancing out of the window, I saw he had them well under control in the vegetable bed.

I remembered that the local Red Cross were holding a jumble sale the following week and I had promised to look out some articles. Anyway, I was glad of the opportunity to have a sort-out in the loft, which could be easily accessed through a door at the top of the stairs. Lots of things had been put up there over the years and I felt a pang of regret when I saw the twins' pram full of baby clothes. I knew Charles wanted a son, but I did not seem to get pregnant again, although we had both seen our family doctor, who saw no reason why I should not have another child.

After working steadily for some time, I soon had a sizable pile for the sale. It was while moving an old Lloyd Loom chair that I came across a small brown suitcase. Snapping open the locks, I saw that it was full of old birthday cards, programmes, newspaper cuttings and letters. A large brown envelope caught my eye. Inside were all James's letters and some photographs – James with his crew, James in uniform taken when he had completed his training and one of him in civvies. My throat contracted as I looked at them. Tears began to prick my eyes as, with trembling hands, I began reading some of the letters.

'My darling Jenny, I love you so,' and 'Only one more op to go, darling, and soon you'll be my wife', I read.

Picking up one of the photographs, all my love for him came flooding to the surface and I was so absorbed that I did not hear Charles come into the loft. It was too late to hide the letters and photos, for they were scattered over the floor. He bent down, putting a hand on my shoulder and looked at the picture I was still holding.

'You've never forgotten him, darling, have you?' he said, softly.

The tears, which had not been far away, began to fall. 'Oh Charles, I'm so sorry. How very silly of me,' I sobbed. 'I'm a respectable, married woman with two children. Much too old to dream.'

'Keep on dreaming, darling,' he murmured, stroking my hair. 'Dreams are precious, but thank you for giving me some of your love.'

Together we put the things back into the case and Charles helped me to take the pile of jumble downstairs, ready for the sale.

I loved Charles in a special way, but knew my love for James was as strong as ever. I still had a strange feeling he had not died on that fateful night. But, suppose one day he did miraculously turn up, what then? I could find no answer to that question.

Chapter Seven

1959

The twins were now twelve years old and attending grammar school. Charles's work kept him busy and we were financially very comfortable.

I had often expressed a desire to visit the bulb fields in Holland, particularly as I was a keen gardener and liked to plant lots of different spring flowers. I was sure I would enjoy the experience.

One day, Charles told me he had arranged such a trip for his mother and me. Ridger would live in and look after the girls, but he was too busy to accompany us at that time. However, a few days before we were due to leave, Charles's mother was called away to look after her sister, who had fallen and broken an arm.

'We'll have to postpone our trip, Charles,' I said, feeling terribly disappointed. 'I'll cancel our reservations straight away.'

'There's no reason why you shouldn't go, darling,' he insisted. 'And anyway the change will be good for you.'

In the end, I agreed and, a few days later, was on my way to the Dutch bulb fields.

The trip was wonderful, the flowers absolutely glorious. Seeing them looking so magnificent, it was difficult to believe that one hundred and forty million bulbs had been consumed by the Dutch population in the terrible hunger winter of 1944–1945.

On the last day in Amsterdam, I went shopping with one of my travelling companions; we were on our way back to the hotel when she decided to go into a small antique shop down a side street.

'I'll wait over there,' I said, pointing to a bench in the sun. I sat there for a while listening to the gay, tinkling tunes of the church bells and then, on an impulse, I got up and strolled over to the antique shop. Although not particularly interested in antiques, I decided to go into the shop. My companion was deep in conversation with the owner so I wandered aimlessly round. As I did so, I noticed a carved, wooden box on a shelf. It was about eight inches long and six inches high.

The carvings on the lid and sides were exquisite, depicting tiny windmills, little Dutch boys and tulips. The box had three small drawers, the knobs for opening them fashioned in the form of tulip petals. I opened the top drawer, which slid out easily. Suddenly, I knew I had to have that box.

'I see you have an eye for a lovely thing,' the shopkeeper remarked when I asked the price.

It was much more than I was prepared to spend, but I felt reckless. 'I'll take it,' I said, impulsively.

As he wrapped it up, he told me that a lady, recently widowed, had brought four such boxes in for him to sell. 'This is the last one,' he went on. 'Her husband used to make them. She's gone to live with her son and his wife. They run a guesthouse in the next village. As a matter of fact, she left a card with me, asking if I would display it in my window to advertise the guesthouse.' He handed me the parcel but, having no room for it in my shopping bag, I tucked it under my arm.

On our way back, we stopped at a pavement café for coffee. I placed my bag on a chair and the parcel on a table. We lingered for some while, then, realising the time was getting on, made our way to the hotel. We had walked some distance when I remembered I had left the parcel containing the wooden box on the café table.

Having retraced our steps, we saw that my parcel was no longer on the table where I had left it. At that moment and for no reason I could explain, the most important thing in my life was getting it back.

'Have you found a parcel?' I asked a waiter. He shook his head. Panic-stricken, I rushed into the interior of the café and found I was in the kitchen. A large figure in white overalls confronted me.

'Please,' I entreated, 'has anyone handed in a parcel?' He grinned and walked away without answering.

'Please,' I shouted at his retreating back. I was frantic.

Then he bent down and took something from a cupboard. When he straightened up and turned round, I saw it was my parcel. Faint with relief, I thanked him several times, much to his amusement.

'You were very lucky,' my companion remarked. 'It's good to know that some people are honest.'

I did not know at the time how lucky I was, or how significant the purchase of that box would prove to be.

It was not until later that I had a chance to sort out my shopping and pack, ready for our departure the next morning. The box, still in its wrapping, lay on the dressing table. I decided to have another look at it and, tearing off the paper, examined it more closely. It certainly was a fine piece of craftsmanship and I could almost visualise the sculptor constructing it with loving care.

Opening the drawers in turn, I found that the bottom one appeared to be jammed. I pulled it gently several times, but it would not budge. There seemed to be something wedged inside, so, taking my nail file, I inserted it in an effort to flatten the obstruction. Gradually, I was able to prise it open a little wider; I saw some crumpled newspaper inside, yellow with age. At last, the drawer opened fully and I could remove the paper. Something was wrapped up inside.

Mystified, I opened it out and was astonished to see two dog tags attached to a rusty chain, the sort of identification worn by all members of the armed services. I wondered how they came to be in the box and, above all, who had been the owner.

When I picked them up, the first thing I noticed was the serial number. There was something familiar about the sequence. I gasped in dismay, remembering the many times I had written that number; then I checked the name. I was not mistaken. There it was, the letters burning into my brain. The name and number were those of James. The tags belonged to James, my James. I sat for a long time, my mind in turmoil.

Who had put them into the box? Where had they come from originally? And was it possible that James was alive, living, perhaps, not far away? What could I do? How could I find out more about them?

Sleep was impossible but, as I tossed and turned, I thought back to the words of the antique dealer. He had mentioned a guesthouse. I wished I had listened more intently. I thought hard. Yes, I had it. The lady who took the boxes in for him to sell lived in the next village. Her son and his wife ran the guesthouse and she had given him a card to put in his window.

I would return to the shop the following morning, take down the address, then cycle to the village and make enquiries of the lady who had taken the boxes in to him.

Rising very early, I dressed hurriedly and went to reception, where I was able to hire a bicycle and also borrow a local map.

I found the antique shop without difficulty. Yes, the card was there in the window. I wrote down the address, then checked the name of the village on the map. It was some distance away and I began to wish I had eaten before setting off.

A young boy pointed me in the right direction when I reached the village and I found the house quite easily.

Propping the bicycle against a wall, I opened the front gate. The garden was full of colour, the lawns well kept. The house was quite large, its windows sparkling in the early morning sun. Crisp net curtains hung, gleaming white, and window boxes blazed, full of brilliant spring flowers.

As I walked up the drive, panic seized me. I felt stupid. What kind of wild goose chase had I embarked on? I thought of Charles. Whatever would he think? I almost decided to return to the hotel, but curiosity forced me on and I found myself lifting the shining brass doorknocker. Nothing happened for a while. Should I knock again? However, as I was about to do so, I heard footsteps coming along the passage; they seemed to belong to someone walking with a limp.

The door opened. Shock rendered me speechless, for there, standing in front of me, was James. Then everything went black and I collapsed on the doorstep.

Chapter Eight

When I regained consciousness, I was lying on a sofa. A woman of about my own age was bending over me.

'Are you feeling better?' she asked, concern written all over her face. 'My husband carried you in here.' She indicated the man who had opened the door to me and who was now standing by the window.

The mists were fading. I began to function normally as, half raising myself, I looked across the room. There was no shadow of a doubt in my mind that he was James but, as I searched his face, he showed no sign of recognition and, with an agonising pang, I realised he did not know me. James had no idea who I was; James had lost his memory. The lady referred to him as her husband. James was married. It was all too much for me to take in and I sank back on to the sofa, confused and mystified.

An elderly woman came into the room, carrying a tray of coffee and a plate of sandwiches.

'Drink this,' she said, kindly, offering me the cup; 'you'll feel better soon.'

Gasping my thanks, I managed a few sips, although my hands were trembling uncontrollably. The coffee was strong and sweet and gradually revived me.

'I'm so sorry to be a nuisance, but I left the hotel rather early without stopping for breakfast.' How could I explain why I had come? I certainly could not mention the dog tags now. Then I recalled they ran a guesthouse. 'I'm returning to England this morning, but came to make enquiries about your terms, as it is possible I may visit again later on.'

The younger woman introduced herself as Gretta; and then she added, 'This is my husband's mother, Anna. I'll give you a card with our terms. We would be pleased to see you at any time.'

Little did she realise that rage and frustration had welled up inside me. How could Anna be James's mother? What a barefaced lie. How had James come to be mixed up with this family? I forced myself to keep calm. What would be the good of revealing James's true identity? He had no idea who I was and I would only look very silly. They might not believe me anyway.

I suddenly remembered the time. 'I must return to the hotel at once,' I said, getting up hastily. 'I leave at one o'clock.'

'Pieter will drive you back.' Gretta spoke kindly, explaining that he had to go into Amsterdam anyway. 'In spite of his artificial leg, he is a good driver, but I'm afraid he doesn't speak English. We've tried to teach him, but he can't seem to pick it up.'

I sat down again. Shock followed shock. James had lost a leg, he could not speak English and his name was Pieter. Oh my God, I thought, my poor darling James. I wanted to cry.

'Are you sure you're fit enough to leave?' Anna asked anxiously.

'Oh yes, thank you. I feel all right,' I told her. Then, as I got up to leave, my glance fell on a silver-framed photograph standing on a small table. I peered at it more closely.

'That is our daughter, Riet,' Gretta said, proudly.

The girl in the picture was a younger edition of her mother. A little on the plump side, blue eyed and fair, with plaits coiled over her head. That was certainly not James's daughter. I felt sure of that. Why, she bore no resemblance to him whatsoever; immediately I resolved that I would never rest until I had unravelled the mystery. I would find out, no matter how long it took, what had happened to cause James to lose his memory. Why was he living in Holland with a woman who called him her husband, and another who claimed he was her son?

I had no idea as to how I would set about my investigations. After all, I was a married woman and had to think of my husband and the children. And how could I tell Charles that I had found James after all these years?

Shaking hands with the two women, I thanked them for their kindness, expressing a hope that I would be able to come again some time.

James was waiting by the car, having already strapped my bicycle on the roof rack and opened the passenger door for me, before getting into the driving seat. The situation was ridiculous. Here was I, isolated in a small space with James: James who had loved me, James who was to have been my husband, yet we were acting like total strangers. I stole a glance at his face, but he was intent on watching the road and conversation was impossible, as Gretta had told me he spoke no English. Unfortunately, my knowledge of

Dutch was very poor, but I vowed I would remedy that as soon as possible.

When we arrived at the hotel, James helped me from the car, then unstrapped my bicycle from the roof rack and wheeled it up to the front entrance. Well, at least that was typical of the James I had known, the James who always possessed such charming manners.

As I thanked him for his help and shook his hand, I saw a puzzled expression in his eyes as though he was desperately trying to remember something, but in a few seconds the look had vanished, and he turned away, limping back to the car.

Back at the hotel and away from the situation, I wondered if it would be more sensible to forget that I had seen James. His wife seemed a kind, caring person. He had a comfortable home and I could not say he looked unhappy. And yet...and yet...I had detected in his eyes a sort of lost look. The whole situation was very baffling. I could hardly believe I had actually spoken to him, touched him.

Would it be better for everyone's sake if I forgot about the events of that morning? Would it be wiser to leave things as they were and not interfere? How could I write and inform his parents, who now lived in New Zealand, that I had seen him but that he had lost his memory, was married to a Dutch girl and living in Holland?

How would Charles react if I told him I had found James and intended to solve the mystery? He would, naturally, be terribly upset and I had no intention of breaking his heart. It was no good; my overexcited brain refused to grapple with the problem further; I filed the matter away, hoping that perhaps an opportunity would arise in the future when I could visit James once more.

Chapter Nine

Charles was at the airport to meet me on my return, grinning from ear to ear. 'Darling, I've missed you so very much. That's the last time I let you go away on your own,' he vowed. Secretly, I pondered on how I would ever be able to return to Holland on my own.

I tried to settle down to normality and, to a degree, I managed quite well, but, always, always, James was in my thoughts, waking and sleeping. Yet my home life, entertaining, the twins, and numerous village activities kept me fully occupied, though sometimes, when sitting quietly in the evening with Charles, listening to our favourite music, my knitting would fall unheeded from my hands and my thoughts would take flight.

Once, Charles asked me why I often looked so pensive. 'Sometimes,' he said, 'since you returned from Holland, you seem such a long way away from me. Did something happen while you were there you haven't told me about, darling?'

Startled by his remark, I had assured him that, of course, nothing had occurred while I was away, but sometimes I had an overwhelming urge to open up my heart and tell him about James. What would be the good though? It would only make him unhappy and unsettled.

The wooden box bought in Holland had been much admired. I had removed the dog tags, stuffing them at the back of my wardrobe inside a pair of red sandals. Charles would never come across them there, but I was wrong for, one evening, as we left to attend a dinner party, the strap of one of my sandals broke. 'Get into the car, darling,' Charles insisted, 'I'll pop upstairs and get your other red ones.'

I leapt out of the car, remembering the dog tags. He would be sure to see them. To my relief, however, when I reached the front door, Ridger, who was looking after the twins for the evening, was handing him the telephone and I had time to fetch the sandals myself.

I had a dread that no matter where I hid the tags, there was a possibility that Charles might, one day, find them, so I decided to take Ridger into my confidence and ask her to look after them for me. I had no intention of getting rid of them in case they were vital in getting James reinstated as a citizen of the UK if he ever regained his memory.

Over coffee next morning, when Ridger and I had the house to ourselves, I told her my story, beginning from the time when, during the war, I had first met James.

She was a good listener and did not interrupt me, though when I gave her an account of the recent events in Holland, she exclaimed in astonishment. Concluding my story, I asked if she would take care of the dog tags for me. 'I'm so worried that Charles might find them one day,' I explained. 'I'd be much happier knowing they were out of the house.'

'Of course I'll look after them for you, Jenny,' she agreed. 'But are you quite sure the man you saw was really James? You couldn't have been mistaken, could you?'

'Oh Ridger, of course it was James,' I answered without hesitation, 'but suppose James's memory returns one day and I don't know about it! I must try to keep in touch with his family. What can I do, Ridger?'

'I suggest you leave things as they are,' was her advice. 'It's strange, but I've often found that things have a way of working themselves out.'

I had to agree with her, but made a secret vow that, one day, I would find a way to return to Holland and see my James again.

Chapter Ten

1959–1960

Christmas would be upon us soon and I was swept up in the usual preparations. That year, we were giving a house party and spent hours decorating the hall and lounge. Charles bought a large Christmas tree, so tall that the top touched the ceiling. I can see his face now as he and Bob Ridger finally got it into position. He was as excited as the twins were and got as much enjoyment in decorating it as they did.

It was such a happy time. Even the weather was seasonal. Snow fell on Christmas Eve, cloaking the trees and shrubs in the garden so that they glistened and sparkled in the moonlight.

That evening, Charles and I lingered after our guests had retired for the night and, as we sipped our nightcap, he took a small parcel from the pile of gifts under the tree, handing it to me, saying, 'I wanted to give you this while we're alone. Happy Christmas, darling,' and he took me in his arms and kissed me.

Inside the parcel was a box containing the most beautiful ring I had ever seen. It was set with rubies and glowed like red-hot coals.

I gasped in delight at the sheer beauty of it. 'Oh Charles,' I exclaimed, 'it's so lovely! I do love you so. You've made me very happy all these years.'

'I've waited a long time to hear you say those words, Jenny. Are you really happy, darling?'

'Yes, Charles,' I answered. 'I really am.' I was happy, I told myself, but deep in my heart a fire still raged and would not be extinguished no matter how hard I tried to quench the flames: a fire that had been lit during the tumultuous years of war and refused to be subdued.

But my life was to change dramatically a few weeks later. January came in cold and wet, followed by hard frosts and I was worried when, one icy evening, Charles had to attend a meeting in the village.

'I'll be back by ten o'clock, Jenny,' he assured me. But, when he had not returned by 10.30, I became concerned.

A ring at the door reassured me. Silly old Charles, I thought, he's forgotten his key again. I never could understand why he kept his door keys separate from his car keys.

Running to open the door, I exclaimed, 'Thank goodness you're home, Charles, I was...' The words died on my lips, for it was not Charles on the doorstep. It was our village policeman.

'May I come in, m'am?' he asked.

'Of course,' I answered, wondering about the purpose of his visit as he followed me into the lounge. Perhaps he had come to sell some tickets for the village pantomime. I knew he was a member of the local drama group.

Then I noticed he looked upset, ill at ease. He kept shifting his helmet from one hand to the other.

'Charles will be in soon, he'll...' but he cut me short.

'I've got bad news,' he said. 'There's been an accident. Your husband…'

'My husband,' I heard myself say in a frightened voice. 'Is he hurt? I must go to him.'

'I'm sorry,' he went on. 'Your husband is dead.'

'But he can't be dead. He only went out for a couple of hours. He'll be home soon, I know he will,' I said, foolishly.

The constable continued speaking, his words sounding unreal. I kept thinking, Charles will be in soon. I went over to the window, drew back the curtains and looked out into the black night. Yes, car lights were approaching down the road. The constable had called at the wrong house. But the car did not turn into our drive and I turned to face the bearer of the terrible news.

'I'm sorry,' he repeated. 'It seems a drunken driver forced him across the road and your husband's car hit a tree. Death was instantaneous.'

I sat down, feeling sick.

'Can I fetch a neighbour?' he enquired.

'Get Ridger, please. You know where she lives.'

After he had gone, I just went on sitting there, cold and lost. How could Charles be dead? Charles, who was always so full of fun; Charles, who had looked like an excited schoolboy a few short weeks ago, fixing the star to the top of the Christmas tree. His pipe and tobacco pouch lay on the table by his chair, his library book open at the page he had been reading just before going out.

It did not take long for Ridger and her husband to arrive. How I would have managed without them, I do not know. They were absolute towers of strength in the weeks that followed and a great comfort to the twins, who were devastated.

I went to see Charles. He did not look dead, just asleep. They told me the impact had broken his neck and, apart from some bruising, there were no other injuries.

Later, our solicitor called and assured me that Charles had made sure I would be financially secure if anything happened to him. 'We've lost a good man in the community,' he said. 'He'll be sadly missed.'

'He was a wonderful husband and father,' I answered, sadly.

Now I told myself, I must gather the threads of my life together. I knew it would be difficult. I missed Charles in so many ways. He was always ready with a joke and a loving arm, when I was downcast. The year that followed was a very sad one for us all.

Chapter Eleven

1961

It was now well over a year since Charles's death and, one morning in late February, when I noticed the bulbs thrusting through the damp earth, I began to think seriously about returning to Holland. I would leave it for a while but, maybe, in a few months' time, I would make plans to go again. However, a letter arrived within the next couple of weeks, which made up my mind for me. An aunt of Charles's had written to invite the twins up to Scotland for Easter, which meant I would be free for a while.

'How about coming to Holland with me?' I asked Ridger. 'We could see the bulb fields and then go to the guesthouse where James lives. I've just got to see him again.'

Ridger was reluctant and undecided. 'I don't think it's a very good idea. You'll only make yourself upset,' she warned. 'You've had enough trouble without going to look for it.'

But, in the end, she agreed and, leaving Bob in charge, we set off. I hired a car so that I could take her around and show her the countryside, though, as the time drew near for our visit to the guesthouse, I felt extremely apprehensive.

'I'm wondering if we should cancel, Ridger,' I ventured. 'Do you think we should?'

'Now that we're here, I think we ought to go, Jenny,' was Ridger's reply. 'If we don't, you'll most likely regret it and never be satisfied until you see your James again.'

So we went.

There was no sign of James when we arrived. Gretta seemed pleased to see us, making us very welcome. 'My husband is in Amsterdam,' she explained, 'and won't be back until this evening. Our daughter is getting married this week,' she went on. 'We would be pleased if you would come to the ceremony and to the reception afterwards in the village hall.'

I could not believe I was going to see James again, but when we met at dinner, he still showed no sign of recognising me, which was as well, as I had no wish to upset the household at the time of their daughter's wedding.

From the start, Anna and Ridger got on well together. They shared common interests – sewing and cooking – and I secretly hoped they might correspond after we returned. That would be a useful link with James.

The day before the wedding was to take place, as Anna and Ridger were busy in the kitchen, I decided to go into Amsterdam on my own but, as I was leaving the house, Gretta suggested that James drive me in as he had several errands to attend to in the town.

It was heaven to be with him and, as my knowledge of the Dutch language had improved, we were able to have at least some sort of dialogue.

On reaching the town, I suggested we have coffee together and he readily agreed. As I picked up my cup, I noticed that he was gazing intently at the eternity ring he had given me all those years ago and which, since my marriage, I had worn on the third finger of my right hand. Suddenly, taking my hand in his, he studied the ring more closely. As he did so, he seemed to be struggling to remember something. Then he switched his gaze to my face, a puzzled expression in his eyes. I held my breath. Was the ring going to be the key which would unlock his memory? But, recollecting himself, he got up abruptly, saying he would pick me up at midday.

My first feeling was one of deep disappointment but, gradually, this gave way to a thrill of happiness, because I felt sure that one day, sooner or later, James was going to regain his memory.

Ridger and I had a wonderful time at the wedding. Everyone was so friendly; the atmosphere one of great happiness. I had met Riet soon after we arrived and liked her right away. She was a jolly girl and made a great fuss of her father. I still could not believe, though, that she was really James's daughter.

After the reception, there was dancing and, to my surprise and delight, the little band began to play the tune that had haunted me for years – 'When I Grow Too Old to Dream'. I quickly looked round for James, but he was in the kitchen, helping Ridger with the washing-up. I ran in and touched him on the arm and asked him to dance with me, just as I had done all those years ago. He shook his head, pointing to his artificial leg.

'Come on,' I urged, pulling him towards me. To my delight, he put down the teacloth and followed me into the hall.

Oh, the bliss of being held in his arms again. He managed quite well, considering his disability and, like the time before, I did not want the music to end. But, if I thought the tune would trigger off a spark in his memory, I was mistaken. When the dance was over, he thanked me very politely, then returned to the kitchen.

Ridger and Anna left earlier than the rest of us. 'Anna will offer your friend a glass of her special brandy before they turn in,' Gretta told me, laughing.

It was late when we finally returned to the guesthouse. Gretta went straight to bed, but I was far too excited to sleep so decided to make myself a hot drink. As I put the kettle on, I was aware that someone had come into the kitchen, clicking the door shut behind them. It was James and suddenly, magically, I was in his arms and he was kissing me hungrily, passionately. We clung together for a long time. Then, 'James, darling, James,' I cried, but, releasing his arms, he took a step back.

'Ik heet Pieter! Ik heet Pieter!' he exclaimed in surprise, then apologising, he turned and left me.

I was utterly bewildered. Was James falling in love with me, not knowing I was his Jenny, unaware that we had met years ago and had planned to marry? Of course, I wanted him to fall in love with me as the Jenny he had previously known. I wanted him to remember his true identity. Had the incident merely been triggered off by a happy day at his daughter's wedding, to be forgotten in the light of day? I went to my room, troubled and confused.

To my surprise, Ridger's bedroom light was still on. 'I thought you would be fast asleep,' I said, popping my head round her door.

'I've been waiting for you to come up,' she answered, telling me to shut the door. 'Come closer,' she whispered.

I sat down on her bed, wondering what all the secrecy was about.

'I've found out what happened to James. I can't go into it now, but tomorrow morning, we'll get away from here and go into town. I'll tell you all about it then. Go to bed now and get some sleep.'

Go to sleep, I thought. How could I possibly sleep when I should soon find out how James came to be living in Holland and what had happened on that fateful night when his plane had crashed. I was in an agony of anticipation, but I must have slept because, when I awoke, I remembered I had been dreaming about a crashing aircraft, smoke and flames belching from the fuselage, and bodies struggling in the water.

Chapter Twelve

The following morning, soon after breakfast, I drove Ridger into Amsterdam. We settled ourselves in the corner of a quiet café and ordered coffee. Then Ridger began her story, an amazing saga which she had heard from Anna after they had returned from the reception. She had suggested that Ridger join her in a glass of brandy and then, taking a family album from a cupboard, had shown her photographs of her own wedding day, the farm she and her husband ran during the war, as well as several photos of her son, her only son, she had explained, in various stages of childhood. Turning a page, she had pointed out a picture of him taken just before the war, when he was eighteen years old. 'Shortly after that was taken he lost his right leg in a tractor accident and then, during the war, he was drowned,' she told Ridger.

On hearing these last words, Ridger had interrupted her. 'Who is Pieter, then? I thought he was your son.'

Anna had hesitated before answering, but warmed and encouraged by the brandy, had related the following story.

During the war, her husband was fishing with some friends when a large force of RAF planes had flown over the Zuyder Zee on their way back to England, a common enough sight in those days. One of the bombers was in trouble, on fire and flying low. One of the crew baled out of the rear turret, but the plane had flown on. They had managed to rescue the airman, who was unconscious, and had hidden him under a tarpaulin.

When they got back to the farm, they examined him, finding that his right leg had been terribly injured, either from an anti-aircraft shell or a blast from a night fighter's gun. He had lost a great deal of blood so they had sent for a doctor working for the Resistance movement. However, the only way to save his life had been to amputate the leg above the knee.

They had hidden the airman in a small attic and, although the Germans, who came to the farm to collect supplies, made checks from time to time, they had been lucky and he had not been discovered.

Very gradually, he had recovered but, by this time, they realised he had completely lost his memory, including his knowledge of the English language.

Anna's husband had removed the dog tags, hiding them under the water butt.

Then the Germans stationed nearby were sent away and another detachment was posted in their place. The people at the farm had become extremely worried in case more thorough searches were carried out, and had contacted the Resistance about moving the airman. However, because of his amputation, they were reluctant to make arrangements for his escape, a hazardous enough venture for a fit man in that part of Holland, but hopeless for someone so disabled.

Their dilemma was solved by an unforeseen event.

It happened that Anna's son and her husband were out fishing one night when a sudden squall capsized their small boat resulting in the son being drowned. His father had recovered the body and, with the help of friends, had taken it back to the farm. It was then that the daring suggestion had been made that the airman take the son's place and stay on the farm. Both were about the same height, both had their right leg amputated above the knee. One problem was the hair colouring. The airman was very dark but Pieter, the son, had light brown hair.

This was overcome by dying the airman's hair; the Underground movement were contacted to carry out small alterations to the son's identity card. The fact that the airman was unable to speak his native tongue was an asset.

The son was buried in secret at the farm. Few people knew of the switch, though Pieter's fiancée had to be told. Their marriage, which was to have taken place later that year, had been brought forward because she found she was pregnant. So it was agreed that she would now marry the airman. This would further allay any suspicions; thus, the two were married and settled down on the farm. Gretta was very kind to him and gradually taught him to speak Dutch.

The Germans frequently rounded up young Dutchmen, sending them away to work in their factories but, because James, now Pieter, lived and worked on a farm which supplied the enemy with food, it was thought doubtful they would ever take him away.

The child, a daughter, had been born six months later. 'So, you see, Jenny,' Ridger concluded, 'Riet isn't his real daughter after all.'

'I think Anna was relieved to tell me her story,' Ridger went on. 'It had been worrying her for a long time. She had felt she ought to report the matter to the authorities after the war, but decided to leave things as they were, particularly in view of the fact that the airman had lost his memory.'

I had been silent all the while Ridger had been speaking, amazed at the story she had unfolded. I was glad to know what had happened to James and I could only feel a sense of deep gratitude to this Dutch family who had risked so much for one of our airmen. How truly brave they were.

'I think it doubtful that James will ever recover his memory,' Ridger remarked.

Not only was I inclined to agree with her, I decided it would be better for everyone if I did not see James again. My decision was a difficult one, but perhaps Ridger would correspond with Anna and that way I would have news of James from time to time.

Chapter Thirteen

1963–1964

We returned home, I very sad, but relieved to know that Anna had promised to keep in touch with Ridger. Although outwardly I settled down fairly well after our visit, I was unhappy to think that James might never recover his memory, might never know his true identity. I wondered if Gretta would be terribly upset if he did remember. Anna had confided to Ridger that, although Gretta was very fond of him, theirs had, of course, not been a love match, but they had been quite happy over the years.

Whenever Ridger received a letter from Holland, she would bring it in for me to read. One morning, she came in with a letter from Anna, saying it contained bad news. 'Oh no! Not James! Don't let it be James,' I prayed.

'It's Gretta,' Ridger told me, unfolding the letter. 'She died in her sleep last week.'

I was shocked. Gretta had seemed so strong, so healthy. I thought of James and wondered how he had taken the loss of his wife. I wanted, with every fibre of my being, to go to him, but knew I could do nothing for a time.

The weeks passed and one day Ridger showed me another letter from Anna, accepting an invitation to come over for a holiday and, joy of joys, James was coming with her.

I waited for the visit in a frenzy of anticipation. Would James, once in England, regain his memory if I stimulated him by taking him to see familiar sights, or would the visit prove a disappointment, ending in his returning to Holland and living there for the rest of his life?

Had he really felt anything for me the night he had embraced me after the wedding? Could I make him fall in love with me even if he never regained his memory? That would be better than nothing. I had to get him back somehow. Surely now that his wife was dead, he would unbend a little and cease to be so remote?

When we met at the airport, I longed to throw my arms round him, but I had to be content with a polite kiss and a handshake.

I was pleased to see that the twins took to him from the start. He seemed to be happy to be with them and, in spite of his disability, played shuttlecock with them on the lawn and table tennis in the conservatory.

We decided that now was the right time to tell Anna we knew James's true identity and that he and I had planned to marry just before he was reported missing during the war. She was overjoyed and amazed, especially when we explained how I had found the dog tags. Her husband, she said, had told her he had removed them from under the water butt after the war, but she had no idea where he had put them. She had become very emotional as, with tears in her eyes, she hoped and prayed that all would turn out well in the end.

I took James to lots of places of interest; sometimes Ridger and Anna would accompany us, sometimes we would go off on our own. One day, I actually drove him to his hometown to the house he once had lived in, but he showed not one flicker of recognition.

We visited the RAF Memorial at Englefield Green and went to London to see the Battle of Britain window in Westminster Abbey and, although he did show some interest, it was obvious that these places meant very little to him.

Was there any other way to trigger off his memory? I asked myself. I was getting desperate and then happened to see, in our local paper, that an air show was being held in the next county. Tomorrow was the final day.

I decided to take James on his own and was delighted to see that he was very interested in all the various types of aircraft exhibited, as well as also in the flying display.

We had covered quite a lot of ground when I saw, over in a corner, an old Second World War Lancaster bomber. I suggested we take a closer look at it. A ramp had been installed, leading up to the door, and I watched as James began to limp along it and then enter the plane. There was something purposeful in his movements.

I followed a short distance behind, my heart beating fast, hardly daring to believe my eyes, for he was making his way, albeit clumsily, to the rear of the aircraft and into the gunner's turret, where he stood gazing out through the perspex canopy. I moved closer, feeling that the rest of my life hung on a tiny thread.

Then he spoke. Spoke in perfect English. 'Skip said to bale out. Oh my God, where am I? Where's my crew? What am I doing here?'

Somehow, I managed to get him out of the turret and back on the ground.

He looked around, wildly. 'Where am I?' He was perplexed and frightened. 'What's happened? Where's my crew?' he kept repeating.

A steward, realising that something was wrong, asked if he could help. Perhaps take James to the first aid post? I declined his offer, saying I could cope. The very last thing I wanted was strangers fussing over him.

I steered him back into the car and, taking his hands in mine, said, 'James, you lost your memory when you baled out of your plane all those years ago. You've been living in Holland with a Dutch family ever since, who looked after you. You married a Dutch girl. They saved your life.'

He looked down at his leg. 'You were injured that night and a doctor working for the Underground had to amputate or you would have died.'

I watched his expression as memory came flooding back.

'What happened to my crew?' he asked.

'I'm afraid they didn't make it,' I said, gently.

'And Jenny, my girl? We were going to be married. Where is she?'

'Oh James, my darling. I'm Jenny. Look at me.' Could we bridge the gap? Would he want me after all this time? Would he recognise me?

Then I saw the last mists clear from his mind as he cried incredulously, 'Jenny, my darling.' We were in each other's arms. How long we clung together, I do not know, but it seemed an eternity – our hearts too full for words.

There was so much to explain but, for the time being, I only briefly outlined the events that had taken place from the time he was reported missing up to the present. I told him about his parents emigrating to New Zealand and that, as soon as possible, we would fly out there and visit them. 'We correspond regularly, but I never informed them that I had traced you. It seemed better not to do so but, by keeping in touch with your Dutch family, I prayed that one day they would tell me that you had regained your memory.'

Ridger and Anna were in the garden when we returned and, on seeing us walking up the path, arms entwined, guessed that all was well and that James had regained his memory. Anna wept tears of joy and, when we related the strange story to the twins, they thought it so romantic, especially when I told them that James and I would be getting married as soon as possible.

It was some time before we were able to make the journey out to New Zealand. James's parents would like to have come over to England right away, but his father had a heart condition and had been advised not to do so.

James and I returned to Holland to settle his affairs and sign the guesthouse over to Riet and her husband. When we explained to her that James was not her real father, she surprised us by saying that she had known all along, but loved him dearly all the same. I had been rather worried at telling her, so I was very relieved.

Anna had to explain to the Dutch authorities about James and James had to get himself reinstated as a citizen of the UK. He also had to convince the Air Ministry that he had indeed been a serving member of Bomber Command all those years ago.

As soon as everything was more or less straightened out, James and I were married very quietly in the little church we were to have been married in, back in 1943.

A few more weeks went by until, at last, the day came when we boarded the plane that would take us to New Zealand.

The lights in the cabin were low. Passengers had settled down for the night. I looked across at the twins. They were fast asleep. James was sleeping too, his head on my shoulder, his hand in mine. I smiled, a little secret smile. I would not tell him yet, but soon I would. Tell him that, when the first roses in our garden filled the air with their sweet fragrance, our child would be born.

Maria

Slowly the sleeping heathered moor
Dims and blurs beneath the stars,
Vacated now by honey bees
Who sipped the golden day away.

Now fragile moths flit through
The soft night air
And moonbeams make a shining halo
Of your dusky hair.

Happy we tread the purple ling,
Our fingers close entwined,
No need for words our love to vow,
It's written in our eyes.

Oh that this night would never pass
And we two here could ever dwell,
Where in the distance I can hear
The salt spray waves lap on the shore,
Murmur your name: 'Maria, Maria.'

But soon these flowers will fade and die
And we too turn to dust, alas,
And others here will roam these paths
To love and laugh the hours away.

Yet oft my soul will ever stray
To this enchanted purple plain,
Where I shall hear again your name,
Crooned on the wind's caressing tongue,
Sighed on the tide as it froths and foams,
That name to me that is so dear,
My darling one, Maria, Maria.

Angels on a Pinhead

*John Donne, a metaphysical poet of the
sixteenth century, suggested one of his
group compose a poem on the subject of
how many angels would fit on the head
of a pin. It is doubtful if this was ever
done. Below is my answer to his
suggestion.*

Mark you this pin that I do hold,
It bears an angel glowing gold;
A tiny creature, 'pon my soul,
With one foot balanced on the head
And on its shoulder, standing straight,
A second angel, arms outspread,
Supports more angels. Up they go,
A pyramid on pyramid
And still they come, a countless throng,
Thousands
Of
Angels
Flying
Down
All balanced on this common pin.

Amazed am I to see them come
To brighten my poor, humble home.

But, suddenly, my trembling hand
Lets fall the pin and, like a cloud,
The angels through the casement fly
In swirling columns to the sky.

It was no dream, of that I'm sure,
For, see here lying on this floor,
A glittering, golden, tiny thing,
A feather from an angel's wing.

Autumn Fires

Flames of autumn lick and quiver,
Curling and crisping spent foliage,
As back garden bonfires cremate,
Consuming summer's excess,
And smoke drifts billowing over
Fallow fields.

Sparks fly, spitting from brittle gorse
And fragile flowers droop, fading
As Summer slows to Autumn's rape,
Leaving the land bleak and bare,
Awaiting frost's veneer.

Yet wait, for even now,
The surge of Spring stirs underground,
Eager for warm, west winds
To resurrect anew.

Fields

Composed after visiting Omaha and
other war cemeteries in France

I have delighted in glorious
Fields and meadows
Filled with corn and blood-red poppies,
Dandelions, daisies, orchids, vetches,
Vigorous, vibrant, burgeoning,
'Mid graceful nodding grasses.

But, with sorrow I have seen
In fields of France
The tombstones white, and crosses
Standing row on row on row
Row on row on row.

Each marks the grave
Of some dear son
That lies to rot and rest,
The cream of youth
Whose blood was spilled,
Fighting the fearsome foe
Long years ago.

And, as I gaze and gaze,
It seems the very air
Is charged with sorrow.

I swear I hear the echoes
Still of warfare;
Feel the horror.

And as the slow tears fall,
I cry for all that wasted youth
Who tasted not the fruits of life,
But spend their time entombed in earth,
Sleeping, sleeping, sleeping,
Leaving the mourners
Grieving, grieving, grieving.

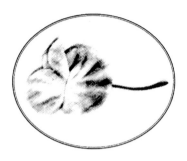

Sweet Peas

Late September
And sweet peas
Still straggle, twining the trellis
Like busy butterflies,
White-, mauve-, blue- and
Pink-winged, trembling
In Autumn's balmy breezes,
Clinging tenaciously.

This morning I have plucked a posy.
Its fragrance delicately
Pervading my room;
But my heart cries
For Summer's demise,
When my fragile flowers
Will fade and die,
Their sweet perfume diminishing
In the chilling air

As their tender blooms
Drop, drifting down
To earth's cold bier.

Peacock

Peacock's feathers – indescribable
when displaying
flamboyant
shimmering
trembling,
Tipped with eye-like spots – iridescent
bronze
blue
green.

Watch him preening
flaunting
exhibiting
round the female.

Hear him shrieking, screeching, clamouring.
See the slow dance
the courtship ritual,
cocky stance.

Dignified, the crested head
now advancing
now retreating

Tantalising
　　　twirling
　　　　　circling
　　followed
　　by
　　　the
　　　　willing
　　　　　female.

One Life

One life is all we have,
One life,
A span of years.

But not for some.
For pestilence, war and famine take their toll,
Abuse of young and old and cruelty across the
    world,
When life, a precious life,
Is stopped up all too soon.

But life should be
To each and every one
A journey of enchantment,
A great adventure,
Where life and all its fruits
Are savoured to the full.

The simple joys of life are priceless –
Who can hear the blackbird's song at dawn,
See drifts of bluebells under shady trees
Or breathe in scent of honeysuckle, rose and
Sweet may blossom
And not feel wonder?
Taste the red wine, the crusty loaf
And not give great thanks?

Work hard with hand and brain and sleep
    refreshed
To wake anew to other days all filled with love
And happy hours.

But, sadly life is not all joy
And not a wondrous journey;
For, some there are who suffer pain and great
Adversity, bereft of love,
When life can be all sadness
And one ponders on the scheme of things
And wonders.

One life is all we have,
One life,
A span of years.

Tempus Fugit

Time, fleeting time, don't run so fast!
In vain I plead with you to pause
Now that my seasons all are spent.
        Does nothing last?

        The clock runs on
        Tick
                            Tock
        Tick
                            Tock

Stop! Stop! Stop! Stop!
  Shut up! Shut up!

Oh time, you avaricious time,
Snatch at my hours and toss them down
Like dead leaves, withering on the ground.

Just once again let me but see
The flambeaux on the chestnut tree,
The pollen-laden bumblebee,
A skein of wild geese on the wing,
The celandine that heralds spring,
White violets peeping through green turf,
The rippling wave, the foam-flecked surf.
Taste hunks of crusty new-baked bread
And wake to blue skies overhead.

Feel sunshine warm caress my skin.
Hear nightingales and blackbirds sing.

But you are deaf to all my pleas
And as you turn and my hand seize
Away from all I hold most dear,
I'm running out of time, I fear,
As, suddenly, you stand stock-still.

       My clock runs down,
       The sunset fades
       The velvet-petalled rose decays;
       My eyes grow dim,
       My senses numb.
And as I draw a faltering breath,
A spectre grim stands in my path.

AND I BEHOLD MY DEATH.

A Strange Romance

I had warned Lyn, my best friend, when she had bought the isolated cottage, two miles from the nearest village. She had only laughed. 'It isn't a good idea,' I had said, 'living in that lonely place on your own.'

'I'll be all right, don't worry,' she had answered. 'Anyway, here I can be assured of complete privacy, free to write without interruption. I have lots of research to do, so I will be away from time to time.'

She refused to have a telephone installed and her nearest neighbours were a mile or so away.

I was to stay with her for a week, but her usual call from the village telephone kiosk, confirming our arrangement, had not come, nor had I received a letter.

When I rang her mother, she informed me that she had not seen Lyn or had a telephone call from her for several weeks. I suggested she may have been away on some research for a book. Her mother did not think so as she felt sure she had already completed the research on her current work.

'I do wish Lyn would meet a nice young man and settle down,' her mother went on, 'but she doesn't seem interested in anyone. She's a strange girl.'

I felt concerned so decided to go up to Poltumley the following day, as arranged.

Turning the car into the drive of Elderflower Cottage, I sighed with relief when I saw Lyn's car in the drive. However, there was no reply when I knocked. She was not in the garden either.

She always kept a key hidden under a certain stone so I unlocked the front door and went in.

There was no sign of her downstairs and, thinking she might be unwell, I went up to her bedroom. The bed had certainly been slept in. It seemed as though she had got up some time during the night, because the bedclothes were thrown back. However, there was no sign of anything sinister. No blood stains. No struggle.

Her disappearance was a mystery. I wondered if she had been sleepwalking, but felt it hardly likely since, if this was so, she would not have locked the door behind her. The French window was also locked in the downstairs room at the back of the house.

I searched in the wardrobe for clues. Her suitcases were still there, as were all her clothes.

My journey had taken some hours and I was tired and hungry. The fridge was empty, which was strange, as I knew she always stocked up when expecting me.

What was I to do? Contact the police and inform them Lyn was missing? That certainly would be the most sensible course of action. Could there be some simple explanation? I thought not.

My head began to ache and a great drowsiness came over me. I lay down on the sofa and, pulling a plaid rug across my body, I fell into a deep sleep.

I must have slept for several hours, waking to find the room flooded in brilliance. It was light enough for me to see the time by my watch. It was 2 a.m. It could not be light from the moon. It was too bright.

Flinging off the rug, I crossed over to the French window, which looked out onto the garden. My first thought was that I must be dreaming. I pinched my arm very hard. It hurt. I was not dreaming. I was surprised I was not frightened. I felt quite calm.

There, standing on the lawn, I saw a machine shaped like a large torpedo and, as I stared in disbelief, a door slid across and two figures emerged. I held my breath. I recognised one of them. It was Lyn in her nightdress. The other was a tall, fair-haired man in a shiny, white suit. Then I heard music, the like of which I had never heard before. It was so beautiful. It brought tears to my eyes. The man took Lyn in his arms and held her in a tender embrace; then he disappeared through the door and the craft began to lift vertically off the ground.

Lyn came running up to the French window, opening it with a key, and stepped into the room. She seemed to sense that I was there, and said, 'Sorry I wasn't in. I've been away for a while. You saw everything, of course? I should have been back two days ago, but the craft developed a problem.'

I had to admit I had seen the craft and she and the man embracing, but before I could ask any questions, she explained that she had met Jarris one night, two years ago, when she had seen his craft land in a nearby field. She had gone across to investigate and their romance had begun from that time.

'We are deeply in love, but can never be together for always. It is enough that we meet at intervals. I am so very happy,' she told me.

Then she looked at me very strangely, a compelling sort of look, and I saw a bright green light flash from her eyes. She's going to destroy me, I thought, because I have seen too much. I would talk. I fell back onto the sofa, trembling violently. I felt dizzy. Then I realised I had been programmed – programmed so that I would never speak to anyone about her love affair with a spaceman.

As though nothing extraordinary had occurred, she suggested we make a pot of tea and catch up with our news, then she would tell me about the book she was working on. Lyn certainly is a strange girl.

Downfall

December's grey waves lashed the tiny dinghy, which was gradually filling with water, the airman's attempts at baling out having little effect. Shot down too far from the British coast to expect rescue, he realised his days were spent, his life bankrupt. He had diced with death once too often.

He thought of his parent's heartache when they received the telegram concerning his death. Born into an aristocratic family, he had been privileged, spoilt – an arrogant young man, a snob, now cut down to size; a miserable scrap of half-dead humanity awash in a hostile environment.

For some strange reason, he found himself thinking of his cockney batman, regretting the ungracious way he had treated him. He could not stand his accent though. His "Ere's a noice cuppa 'ot Rosie Lee' when he woke him every morning grated on his nerves. Why could the man not speak properly?

Utterly exhausted, he tried to feel in a pocket for some barley sugar, but his fingers, paralysed with cold, were useless.

Then, above the sea sounds, he heard the throb of an engine and, looming out of the mist, the advancing shape of an RAF Air Sea Rescue launch. Strong arms grabbed him. Someone shouted in his ear: 'Cor blimey, mate, wot a day ter go larkin' abart in the Norf

Sea. Bet yer couldn't 'arf do wiv a noice cuppa 'ot Rosie Lee'.

The words he might, one day, forget; the dialect he would respect forever.

Pandemic 1918-1919

It started in America
And later reached Samoa,
The dreaded influenza
Beginning in September,
Which raged across the universe.

Even the fit and healthy fell
To this mysterious disease –
No virus was discovered.
When dead bodies were examined,
The virus had quite vanished.

Inoculations held no hope,
The fit and healthy suffered most,
Yet many soldiers in the trenches
Escaped the awful sickness;
It was a mystery.

All life was disrupted
Because so many were affected,
And coffins in such short supply
Were looted.

It's true that Woodrow Wilson
Came to the conclusion
That this could be
The end of civilisation.

Nearly forty million languished,
More than two and twenty million perished.

But alas no trace survived
For the scientists to arrive
At a definite diagnosis.
It was a mystery, a tragedy,
An unsolvable enigma.

Sunflower Fields (France)

Field upon field
Of
Sunshine flowers
Sunflowers
Single-stemmed
On foliage
Dark
Dense
Standing tall
Aloof
Heavy-headed
Sea of faces
Glowing
Glaring
Gazing sunwards
Sun worshippers
Each one
Reflecting
A little sun
Wearing
Bonnets frilly
Yellow-petalled
Circling centres
Bronzed
Bursting
Seed-full
Nutritious

Delicious
Kernels
Source of oils
Heart of gold
Majestic beauty
King of flowers
Golden-crowned
Sunshine flowers
Sunflowers.

Where Have All the Meadows Gone?

Last night I had a dream
That someone stole the meadows,
Thieving all the hedgerows,
Making off with all the flowers
So that nothing now remained
Of quiet country lanes;
The streams we used to fish in
For tadpoles and for tiddlers
Obliterated –
But it was just a dream,
Or so it seemed
Till I awoke and heard
The sound of busy bulldozers
Demolishing the meadows,
And my dream became a nightmare
As concrete mixers spun,
Spewing out their contents
For avenues of houses,
Desirable residences,
Four bed, two bath, three loos, a shower or two,
With regimented gardens
And billiard-table lawns.

Now nothing's left of all the meadows,
No dog rose-tangled hedgerows,
No buttercups or daisies
In disorderly confusion

Among sweet-smelling grasses
Or copses full of bluebells.
But a disobedient dandelion,
Rooted deep in concrete,
Refusing to be buried
Is screaming condemnation
At the plunder and the pillage
And the death of all the meadows
Where the rabbits used to run
And linnets softly sung
When I was young.

Soubes

Southern France, June

Old houses huddled high on a hill,
Clinging in solid embrace.
Sombre alleyways echoing still
With murmurs of bygone days.
Few sunbeams filter in between,
But, against the old stone walls,
Blazing geraniums gaily bloom,
Piercing the grey and shadowy gloom.

But, out on the hills that circle the town,
Fragrant broom bushes wear glittering crowns.
Brilliant blue butterflies skim the wild flowers
And cherries hang mellow in clusters
And grapes on the vine show promise of wine
And borne on the breeze is the scent of wild
    thyme.
Leaves on the olive trees shimmer like silver
And gurgling water
Gushes
And
Splashes
From
Green-fronded grottos.

Green lizards lie basking asleep in the sun
And nightingales sing all afternoon long
In Soubes.

Autumn Crocus

When I was a child I planted a garden,
A garden of love,
And I filled it with violets, forget-me-nots,
    daisies
And sweet-scented lilies and primroses, pansies –
Then, when a maid, I sewed sunny marigolds,
Bright blue delphiniums, cornflowers, poppies,
Exciting brilliant vibrating posies;
And later I planted bushes of roses,
Creamy white roses, bridal-white roses,
Pure fragrant blossoms among all my flowers,
Then added an archway, an archway of ramblers,
Scarlet-red ramblers scrambling like children.
My garden ran riot, a confusion of colour,
A garden of love forever and ever.

But frosts of Autumn came one day
And took my lovely flowers away.
The earth lay bare, love's fire burned low,

Safely smouldering, under control –
Till yesterday, raking through dead leaves
I spied an Autumn crocus gleam
And, in my heart, it lit a flame
And my garden bloomed with love again.

You Wouldn't Dare

(In Memoriam)

I'll never forget and I'll always regret
That you never dared marry me.

'Why can't we be wed?' I often said,
And you answered, 'I just don't dare –
I might be disfigured, blinded, disabled,
Or leave you widowed; that's why I'll never
   dare –
And what if I'm killed and you bear our child?
No, darling, it wouldn't be fair.'

'But I don't understand, my dearest one,
I really just don't see,
If you brave the Hun and the Messerschmitt's
   gun,
Why you don't dare marry me?
What is it you feel for the hard, grey steel
Of that Lancaster loaded with bombs?
Surely the only thing that's real
Is the warmth of my loving arms.'

So did you think of me when they holed your
   kite
And you ditched in the Zuyder Zee?
And as you tossed in the cold green troughs

And the waves washed over your head,
Did you curse because you never dared,
Dared to marry me?

And now it's too late
And I'll never forget
And I'll always regret
You didn't dare marry me.'

Ten-Minute Walk

'It's only a ten-minute walk from the bus,
You're sure to find it without any fuss.'
So when I arrived at my destination
I walked up the High Street without hesitation,
But after a period of ten whole minutes
I could find no trace of a house called The
    Linnets,
So I asked a local out riding a bike
Who shouted across to a man called Mike,
'Oi, Mike, know where The Linnets is, mate,
Cos I ain't never seen that name on a gate?'
Mike took off his cap and scratched his head:
'I don' rightly know, m'dear,' he said.
'It ain't round here, of that I'm sure.
Do yer know the colour of yer friend's front
    door?'
'Oh no, I've never been here before
So I don't know the colour of their front door.'
'Go and knock up the vicar, 'e's sure ter know,
'E'll tell yer exactly where ter go.
The church is on'y along Pine Way,
A ten-minute walk or so I should say.'
So I knocked up the vicar who had no idea.
'I really cannot help you, my dear.
That name to me doesn't ring any bells.
Wait there, I'll just go and ask one of my gals.'
But when he returned I could see by his face

His gal didn't know, but suggested Miss Grace,
A spinster living nearby in The Chase,
Might know of a house called by that name,
Which she did, saying, 'Go up the end of that
    lane;
It's about a mile on; turn left at Home Farm.'
With a sigh of relief I set off again
And certainly found when I got past the farm,
A house called The Linnets, but no one was in
    it.
'They've gone off to Spain,' a neighbour
    informed me,
'And won't be returning until next February.
I'd ask you in for a cup of tea
But I suffer greatly from rheumaticky knees.
You'll get a cup at The Dog and Pot.
It's good and strong and nice and hot.'
So thirsty and tired I wended my way –
That ten-minute walk took me half a day.

Easter Walk

Wandering green hills on Easter Eve
As harsh winds scourged the leafless trees,
I saw a dead elm and a wreath
Of golden gorse, a crown of thorns
And violets purple, piercing, bruising turf.
Then heard a cry, a dreadful cry,
And dark clouds hung across the sky.

A silence fell, profound and deep,
And I could only stand and weep
For some deed that had taken place
Long years ago, a kind of death.

But suddenly the sun broke through
And under cloudless skies of blue
Skylarks rose high in joyful song,
Triumphantly exalting,
Proclaiming resurrection.

Death of the Mountains

(Spain)

We, the everlasting hills
        Are
        Disintegrating
        Crumbling
        Fracturing
        From mutilation.
You could call it amputation,
Our life force draining –
We are monstrosities
                Jutting
                Stark naked
                Scarred
                Disfigured.

They are carting us away
Bit
        by
                bit
Stone deaf to our groaning,
To embellish other hills
With icing sugar villas
And swimming pools
Where once the sweet grapes grew

Terrace
        upon
                terrace
And trees of almond flourished
And rosemary ran riot.

We, the everlasting hills
        Are doomed
        Expiring
        Decaying
        Dying,
Dying
        an
            untimely
                    death.

The Bombshell

'I'm leaving,' she announced suddenly on that fateful day.

He stared aghast. 'Leaving! After all these years?'

'Yes, George. Our marriage is over. I want something more out of life. Holidays abroad, a bigger house. You're just a plodder; never get promotion. I'm going to live with Harry. He's going to buy a villa in Spain.

'I want a divorce. We're going to get married. You bore me, George. You should have married someone like Anthea Jones at the library. She's your type – dull, uninteresting. My mind's made up, so don't try and stop me.'

George, a mild-mannered man, already showing signs of a slight stoop so that he looked older than his forty-five years, wore a time-imposed, perpetual frown, reminding one of a spaniel eager to please his master. The frown deepened at his wife's outburst. She had taken him completely by surprise. Normally a slow thinker, he was now utterly at a loss for words. He visibly sagged.

They had got on all right together over the years, he supposed, and although they could do with a bit of extra money, he had never nagged Sally because she refused to get a job. Although childless, with plenty of time on her hands, she seemed to spend a great part of her day lounging around reading trashy thrillers and romances. He never raised any objection when she went off on her own on Saturdays with friends, or asked questions when she sometimes stayed out all night. As for Harry, a travelling salesman, by all accounts – a bit of a philanderer, he imagined.

He had reminded her many times that when his elderly aunt died, he would come into some money, but she had only scoffed. 'Don't kid yourself that old girl will leave you anything. She only says she's left her money to you so you'll keep visiting her. The cats' home will get everything, mark my words.'

By the time he had formulated some sort of reply to her outburst, she had turned on her heel and clattered upstairs. He heard her flinging the wardrobe doors open and dragging suitcases across the floor. She really meant it, then.

The situation was beyond him and, sighing heavily, he went off into the garden and busied himself deadheading the roses.

When he returned from work next day, she had gone. At first the house seemed quiet without her but, gradually, he began to enjoy being on his own. He had not realised just how much she nagged him. Nice to eat his breakfast in peace without being disturbed by Sally shouting from the bedroom every few minutes for tea, the newspaper; or complaining that the toast was burnt.

He wondered why he had ever married her. Funny, but he had never given it much thought before. She had been a pretty, petite blond but rather silly. Her tongue had always been razor sharp; never satisfied, although he worked hard to provide a comfortable home and make her happy.

When the divorce papers came through, he did not contest and was relieved to know he was a free man.

However, as time passed, Sally realised that living with Harry was not as much fun as she had thought it would be. He never mentioned marriage, even after the divorce. He did not seem to have a regular job either. She suspected that he and his mates operated dangerously near the limits of the law. He gambled heavily. Sometimes money was plentiful, but often he was hard up.

She had been forced to find work, but then he borrowed from her and she considered herself lucky if he paid her back. His friends, heavy smokers and drinkers, filled the tiny flat with their raucous talk. He was always wanting her to go to the pub, or to go dancing and to nightclubs. She was tiring of it all, not least his incessant sexual demands.

Gradually she admitted to herself that she had made a big mistake. Harry was never going to marry her. She did not want him now, anyway. As for his promise to buy a villa in Spain, that was a laugh. The nearest they had got to that had been a long weekend in a crumby apartment in Benidorm. If she left him, he would very soon find another companion.

She wondered how George was managing. She had neither seen nor heard anything of him since leaving and she had never bothered to keep in touch with anyone from the village she had left. How she missed the pretty garden, which George tended so carefully and where, on sunny days, she enjoyed sunbathing.

The small flat she shared with Harry got on her nerves.

Suddenly her mind was made up. She would return to old George. He would welcome her with open arms. Good, stolid old George. How pleased he would be to see her! Lovely to have her breakfast in bed again instead of getting up first and waiting on Harry. He was going up north with a couple of his pals on the following Friday, negotiating some shady deal, she suspected.

After he had gone, she would pack all her belongings, leaving the suitcases in the hall for George to collect. Harry would not come after her and make trouble; at least she hoped not.

It was midday when she arrived at her destination, feeling happy and carefree. The day was warm and sunny and so, instead of taking the local bus, she decided to walk. As she reached the church, the bells started to ring. A gleaming-white Mercedes, decorated with pink ribbons, was drawn up in front of the lynch gate. Sally had a thought. She and George would marry again, but this time the ceremony would take place in the church, not in a registry office as before. She would wear a blue silk suit with matching hat. Perhaps even a short veil.

Full of happy thoughts, she lingered in the warm sunshine. Now the bridal pair were coming through the lynch gate, the bride looking lovely in a froth of pink lace, the groom immaculate in morning suit. She edged nearer. It was then that she suffered the worst shock of her life, for the groom was none other than George.

'George! George!' she muttered hoarsely, her hands flying to her mouth to suppress a scream.

Hardly believing her eyes, she saw before her a transformed George. Gone was the drab, colourless individual she had left two years ago. This man seemed taller, poised, years younger. The hangdog expression had vanished. He positively glowed with happiness.

Her thoughts in a turmoil, she leaned against the hedge for support. As the Mercedes drove away, an usher called to her.

'Groom's side?' he asked.

'No,' she answered, disappointment, jealousy and frustration welling up inside her, bitter as gall. 'No,' she repeated, turning away. 'I never knew George, never knew him at all.'

Branston

She wasn't our dog
But belonged to our daughter,
Though we often looked after her.

Sue got her from Ascot,
From a dog rescue centre
Where she'd been taken
By her owner, a publican
Who retired to a flat
So couldn't keep Branston.

She was the champion beer swiller
In the south-west of Dorset –
Perhaps she'd been weaned
On bowls of draught beer!

Her manners were perfect,
Such a dignified dog
When walking to heel;
Never distracted, so protective,

We always felt safe and secure
With our Branny.

Quite a large dog, a sort of retriever
But her tail an Alsatian's,
Her coat glossy black
With a sprinkling of ginger.

She loved being groomed,
Liked jumping in water,
Chasing thrown sticks
And playing with balls,
Being tickled and cuddled.

A bit of a coward if cows were about
When she'd skulk close behind us,
Creeping along.

I was sad when I noticed
The weight of her years
On her dear greying muzzle,
Her brown eyes so bleary –
Dear Branny was weary.

Then one day she took sick
And couldn't stand up;
She'd suffered a stroke
So the vet had to inject
And put her to sleep.

How we all miss you, Branny;
Such affection you gave us
And though you weren't our dog

But belonged to our daughter
We often looked after you –
We loved you, dear Branny;
You were the best.

Stolen Fruit

Miss Euphrasia Jane Longstaff arose at her accustomed hour of 6 a.m. to July skies as blue as periwinkles. I shall pick the blackcurrants today, she told herself.

Following her usual daily routine, she knelt by her bed in prayer, then cleansed her body in a bath of cold water, both habits acquired during her many years at the convent whence she had been hurriedly dispatched at the age of twelve years, after being caught frolicking, stark naked, with thirteen-year-old Piers Parnell-Smith among the raspberry canes. Punishment had been swift and painful and Miss Euphrasia, now in her thirty-eighth year, had never again tasted forbidden fruit.

The convent had been her home for many years, her parents having taken themselves off to an obscure part of Africa to do good works among the natives and, eventually succumbing to some equally obscure disease, had left their daughter well provided for so that she had been able to purchase a cottage with a large garden, spending her time between the latter and endeavouring to improve the morals of the younger generation in the nearby hamlet.

As though to mortify the flesh, she enveloped her body in long cloaks – black in winter, brown in summer. Her ramrod frame, topped with flaming red hair screwed into a tight bun, resembled an elongated hatpin. Her sharp tongue and fierce mien had such an effect on the villagers that no one dared to cross her. Whatever she said was gospel and if Miss Euphrasia said black was white, then that was so. In short, all, including the vicar, stood in awe of this fearsome lady.

On this particular morning, Euphrasia ate a frugal breakfast, then donning an old sunbonnet, took several containers from a cupboard and made her way to the kitchen garden. A voice startled her. Turning, she saw a young man, a stranger to those parts, swaggering up the garden path.

'Got any jobs you want doing, lady?' he called to her. His voice was soft, pleasant on the ear and, as he drew nearer, she noticed that under a mop of tousled, black hair, his handsome face was burnt brown by the sun. Gold rings dangled from his ears. His eyes, flecked with amber specks, tickled her memory. They reminded her of the shady trout pool in the woods of her childhood home.

Any other day she would have told him to be on his way, for she would have no truck with peddlers or odd job men, but she hesitated and the sharp rebuke remained unuttered.

Surprising herself, she handed him two large bowls. 'You can pick blackcurrants,' she answered sourly, scowling at him.

As he took the containers from her, their fingers touched and she experienced an odd sensation as his eyes flashed insolently over her body.

He seemed to know where the fruit bushes grew for, showing no hesitation, he led the way to the far corner of the kitchen garden.

They picked steadily for some time, no word passing between them, Euphrasia being so absorbed in her task that it was not until he asked for a glass of water that she remembered his presence.

For the second time that day, she surprised herself because, instead of filling a water jug, she took from the rack a bottle of elderflower wine, which she placed with two glasses on a tray, and carried into the garden.

The gypsy – for she was sure he came from the temporary encampment a mile or two down the road – showed no surprise when he saw the wine bottle. He had taken off his shirt. His chest, covered in dark, curly hair tipped with gold, glistened with sweat and, as he took the glass form her, she could feel the warmth of him.

From overhead, the sun sent down piercing stabs of heat. The air vibrated, full of insect sounds.

'Make this yourself, did you? It's good,' he remarked, wiping his lips with the back of his hand. She nodded, refilling their glasses.

The wine and the heat, combined, were beginning to affect her senses and, yet again, she became painfully aware of his warm body and his close proximity.

'Hot, isn't it? Why don't you take off your clothes?' she heard him murmur softly as he moved even closer.

Her head felt queer, light as a feather. She seemed to be inside a sort of kaleidoscope, where the colours of the summer sky, the juicy fruit and the sunburnt face of the gypsy combined with the shimmering heat haze to whirl her round and round and round. Vaguely she recalled the young Piers fondling her among the raspberry canes all those years ago; the soft whiteness of his man-child body, his immaturity, so unlike this man, tanned, muscular and hard.

Gentle hands eased her out of the faded cotton frock, her petticoat and underclothing. He unpinned her hair so that it fell in luxurious red ringlets round her shoulders. Then he too lay naked beside her.

Now she was swaying, powerless to resist under his spell, moving rhythmically as he caressed her. In her head, star shells seemed to be bursting and subsiding, then everything became a blur and she fell into a deep sleep.

It was some time before she awoke to find the gypsy gone and half the yield of fruit. She had no recollection of taking off her clothes, but the intense heat did peculiar things to one, she mused as she dressed, then took the remaining berries into the kitchen ready for picking over prior to making jam.

As time passed, people remarked on the change in Miss Euphrasia. Her cheeks filled out; her lips were less tightly compressed. They were surprised to see that she now wore her hair loose so that it cascaded like a rippling stream down her back. But she was still Miss Euphrasia Jane Longstaff, a force to be reckoned with.

The following year, when trumpeting daffodils heralded the arrival of spring and vulgar-hued polyanthus shrieked at the cornflower-blue sky, Miss Euphrasia wandered into her garden to inspect the new shoots on the blackcurrant bushes. Suddenly, she gave a sharp scream, clutching her back, then staggered to the telephone.

Later that day, Hope Charlotte was born and, when Euphrasia wheeled her into the village for her first airing and told everyone she had found the child under the blackcurrant bushes, no one dared disbelieve her.

School Days are the Best Days!

I started school at five years old;
'Now always do as you are told,' said Mum.

At first they gave me plasticine
In colours red and brown and green.
Oh, how I hated plasticine
In colours red and brown and green!
It had a nasty horrid pong
And things I moulded turned out wrong.
I couldn't even make a mouse
But Helen Harvey built a house
And got a shiny golden star,
But teacher just said, 'Um' and 'Ah'
At my absurd creation.

One day while learning ABC,
Picking up the letter T,
I tickled Tommy on his knee,
But got a nasty stinging slap
From teacher.
'We don't do that to little boys.
You really do surprise me, Joyce.'
I couldn't see what I'd done wrong –
I only meant to have some fun
With Tommy Dunn.

'I don't like school,' I said to Mum,
It really isn't all that fun
Now I can't play with Tommy Dunn.'
'You must like school, my girl,' she said;
'School days are the best days,
The best days of your life.'

But then things went from bad to worse –
Someone on me had laid a curse,
For when I saw the school optician,
He said I'd got a stigmatism
And very lazy was one eye.
A shade of black he made me wear
For two whole years, I do declare,
And spectacles with silver frames.
Oh, how I suffered horrid names!

For Christmas plays they always chose
A blonde and pretty girl called Rose.
I thought some angels had a fringe
But I was never given wings.
'Your hair's so straight and much too dark,
You'll be a shepherd boy called Mark,
And wear a jacket made of skin.'
But how I hankered after wings!

I never was much good at knitting
And oft was dragged to Nora Gitting
For to see *her* perfect knitting.
How I hated Nora Gitting.

At sports and games I did my best,
But never could beat all the rest
Because my legs so short and plump
Could not over hurdles jump.
And when at netball I did play,
The long-legged girls got in my way
And tripped me up and there I'd lay,
Showing my wincey knickers grey.
'Try harder, dear,' Miss Smith would say.
'Think of our motto truly taught:
'*I am, I can, I will, I ought.*'

I tried so hard to learn to spell,
But found that learning was pure hell,
And teacher always said, 'You know,
In the uptake you are slow.'

On Fridays I liked silent reading
And after prayers the whole school singing
'He who would valiant be.'
Then home and angel cake for tea.

As time went on with boys I'd loiter
Till teacher said to Mum, 'Your daughter
Must not with the boys be seen
Playing on the village green.'
So up in treetops very high
I'd climb with Tom and John and Guy.
Far away from prying eyes –
Till Minnie Morris followed me
And told her mum, who told my mum,
Who told my teacher – jealous creature!

Then one day to my surprise
They said I'd got the English Prize
And my head swelled to twice its size.

Then came the day, oh happy day,
When I my satchel threw away!
School days were finished, over, done:
Now life begins, I thought. What fun!
But soon I came to realise
Amid the world of toil and strife
That school days were the best days,
The best days of my life.

Woodland Walk

If you walk in the woods on a morning in May
Along sun-freckled pathways
Where trees form an archway,
A filigree archway of beech leaves and larches,
And you stand very still
Not making a sound,
You will hear the soft crackle
Of Spring all around
As bracken unfurls
And wild flowers uncurl
And you may see the flash of a gossamer sash,
Hear velvety laughter
Like rippling water
As a wood nymph flits by,
Dusting the grasses with tender birds' eyes.
And as you pass on
You will hear the low whisper
Of warm summer breezes
Caressing the young leaves
Of beech, ash and sycamore.

But be very careful –
Don't leave any traces
Or pluck at the flowers.
Leave the wood as you found it
For the pleasure of others
On future May days.

Snowflakes and Roses

Cruel winter returned to my garden today
Right in the very middle of May;
When some snowflakes fell,
Christening the roses,
Each velvety petal was full of surprises
Bejewelled, full of diamonds
Sparkling and shimmering
Under a spring, blue sky.

But soon midday's sun
Wilted the flowers, stealing the diamonds,
And all that is left of my early May roses
Are faded, bruised blossoms
Staining the soft earth red.

The Night-Wind Fairies (I)

When Amy awoke it was still dark. Something must have disturbed her. She listened. The wind was worrying the twigs of the wisteria growing against the house wall so that some of them tap-tapped incessantly on the windowpane. She was not sure whether it was still Christmas Eve – or was it now Christmas Day? If it was Christmas Day then all her presents would be downstairs round the tree and her stocking filled.

She crawled to the bottom of her bed. Yes, her stocking bulged and rustled when she prodded it. It must be Christmas Day.

Flinging on her pink dressing gown and furry pink slippers, she padded across the floor, opened her bedroom door very carefully and tiptoed downstairs, then softly turned the handle of the sitting room door.

She gasped at the sight that met her eyes. The Christmas tree lights were on and, in the moonshine streaming in from the window, lots of fairies were flying round and round, some swinging from shimmery tinsel festooned over the branches of the tree, others playing leapfrog over the coloured baubles, while several were turning somersaults over the big, gold star on the top of the tree. Amy laughed with delight to see how pretty they looked. Their wings sparkled and glittered so that they seemed like darting fireflies.

'What are you doing here and how did you get in?' Amy asked one of the fairies, who just then flew past her nose.

For answer, the fairy laughed – a little bell-like sound – and all the other fairies joined in. 'We are the night-wind fairies,' they chorused.

'I wish I could fly like you,' Amy said and no sooner had she spoken than she felt herself becoming smaller and smaller until she was the same size as the fairies.

'But I haven't got any wings,' she complained. 'How can I fly without wings?'

A nearby fairy fluttered down and whispered in her ear. 'Go and see old Grimblekin over there. He will make you some wings.'

Amy glanced across the room and there, sitting cross-legged on the edge of her father's armchair, was a tiny elf dressed in red. On his head he wore a pointed cap, which had a yellow tassel on top. Under his dark, bushy brows, his eyes twinkled merrily. A pair of horn-rimmed spectacles was balanced on the tip of his nose.

Two fairies lifted Amy up beside him. She saw that several fairies were sitting along both arms of Grimblekin's chair. They were swinging their legs to and fro impatiently as they waited for the elf to mend their wings, for she saw that they were full of holes.

'Please could you make me some wings?' she whispered.

He eyed her over his spectacles. 'Make you some wings, make you some wings? What have you done with yours, eh? You fairies are a careless lot. How can you lose wings?'

'Please. I've never had any wings,' Amy stammered. She was a tiny bit frightened of him.

'Never had any wings, never had any wings? Dear, dear, dear. Oh well then, in that case...' and he began rummaging through a tiny workbasket, bringing out some fragments of gossamer in brilliant colours. 'What colour, eh? What colour? Be quick, I haven't got all night.'

'I'd like that colour to match my dressing gown, please,' Amy answered, pointing to a pretty, pink scrap of material. 'And could you weave some of the gold thread into it?'

'What a fussy fairy, what a fussy fairy,' Grimblekin grumbled as he set to work.

Amy watched, fascinated, as he took a little pair of scissors and skilfully cut out the shape of wings; then, threading a length of silver thread, he stitched so fast that she could hardly see the needle going in and out of the fabric. He re-threaded his needle with gold, weaving it back and forth and, in no time, the wings were completed.

'Turn round, turn round, don't fidget, don't fidget,' and very deftly he sewed the wings in place on the back of Amy's dressing gown. 'Off you go then, off you go,' and he pushed Amy so violently that she slipped off the chair – yet wonder of wonders, she did not fall, but was suspended a few inches above the floor.

'I can fly, I can fly!' Her words came out like the tinkling of a bell.

Oh, what fun she had sliding up and down the branches of the tree, soaring up to the big, shiny star, then diving down to all the brightly wrapped gifts under the tree and playing hide and seek among the crackers. The fairies did not seem to mind one bit that she was still wearing her pink dressing gown and furry slippers. She would have liked a sparkly dress like the other fairies, but she did not have the courage to ask Grimblekin to make her one.

As time went on, she saw that the fairies were beginning to settle on the branches of the tree and, one by one, were falling asleep. Grimblekin was fast asleep too, curled up in the armchair.

'I'm so very tired, I think I'll go back to bed,' said Amy as she gave a big yawn. Magically she gradually got bigger and bigger until she was her normal size. Quietly she climbed the stairs and was soon cuddled down in her little bed and fast asleep.

'You are a sleepy head,' she heard her mother say as she awoke. 'We thought you would have been down long before this. Happy Christmas, darling,' and she gave Amy a big kiss.

On her way to the dining room, Amy peeped into the sitting room. Everything was as usual. No fairies; and Grimblekin with his tiny workbasket had vanished.

'Can't think how those tree lights got left on,' her father said while they were having breakfast. 'I could swear I switched them off before going to bed. You didn't come down later and switch them on, did you, Amy?'

'No, Daddy, I expect it was the night-wind fairies. They were here and Grimblekin made me some beautiful pink wings.'

'Really, dear,' her mother remarked. 'That was nice of him; now eat up your breakfast.' And she continued trussing the turkey.

'I'm going to open some of my presents, Mummy.'

Amy ran into the sitting room. She looked at the tree, in imagination reliving the scene of the previous night when the fairies had frolicked. She sighed, then cried out in astonishment, for there, on the tip of a branch suspended by a golden thread, was a tiny pair of gossamer wings. Carefully removing them and holding them in the palm of her hand, she ran to her mother.

'Look, Mummy, look! The night-wind fairies have left me my beautiful wings – the wings that Grimblekin made for me.'

'How very kind of him, dear,' her mother answered. What a vivid imagination the child had, she thought as she put the Christmas pudding on to steam.

Celandines

Alas, the blazing daffodils
Have trumpeted their last few trills,
Their brief stay here is over:
'Sic transit gloria'.

The tulips still are at their prayers,
The polys fading fast,
But overnight, or so it seems,
Clusters of shining celandines
Illuminate the flowerbeds,
The grass and shingle drive –
Ubiquitous.

They come so surreptitiously
As though the stars above
Had showered the earth
With angel dust
To compensate us for the loss
Of golden daffodils.

And just as swiftly as they come,
They steal away when summer's sun
Awakes the early rose
And bids laburnum weep
And droop her flaming locks.

But when the blackbird builds in spring
And April bursts in showers of rain,
They'll gild the garden once again,
Sweet celandines benign.

A Dream Visit

From the cold, grey sea,
From the deadly depths,
In my dream you came
From the slime, green shell
Of your turreted hell
In the dead bomber's womb
From your undersea tomb.

I have waited so long,
My darling one,
Since you fell to the gun
Of the murdering Hun,
But at last you are come.

And I take you between
My frost-white sheets
And I kiss your cheeks
And your ice-cold lips
As you melt in my arms.

So long, I murmur,
So long have I waited
And now you are come,
My darling one.

And I was glad that the
Furrows and folds of my years
Were hid under night's covers.

But when dawn's early light
Flooded into the room,
You rose up and left me
And went back to your tomb,
Your turreted tomb
In the dead bomber's womb
In the undersea gloom.

When will you...come again...my love?
When will you...come...again?

Daisies

Winter – and frost's icy finger
Starches hedges, trees and grasses,
Silvering bare landscapes.

Few flowers bloom, but here and there
Like fallen stars on close-cut lawns
The daisy flower defies the storms.

Each little disc a golden sun
Enclosed in frilly, snowy collar,
Demure and dainty.

And as I stand a while and gaze,
My mind goes back to other days
Long gone, when, as a happy child,
I trod the sunny, daisy fields
And wove long chains of nature's jewels.

Sweet daisies thriving
In the frost and snow,
You lift my heart and on it
Cast a joyful glow.

Wedding Dress

There it hangs, my bridal gown,
Nearly as good as new,
Though 'tis years since as a bride
I trod proud and starry-eyed
Down the flower-decked aisle.

The fabric came from London Town,
From a posh department store,
Several yards of taffeta
In pristine white – a sheer delight;
No guilty qualms I bore.
My father saw to that!
A virgin bride – just fancy,
At three and thirty years!

A seamstress living hereabouts
Made up the taffeta –
A princess line,
A sweetheart neck,
Long sleeves that tapered to the wrist
And a bow of blue inside a seam;
Then just for luck from out her head,
She plucked a single hair
To finish off the hem.
It really was a dream.

A dainty veil was garlanded
With flowers of the spring,
And in my hands I carried
A bouquet of pure-white blooms
Presented by my groom.

The bill for making up the dress
Was only just two pounds;
The buffet seven and six a head
And the Honeymoon Hotel
In Eastbourne Town
Cost under thirteen pounds
For seven whole days –
Didn't we do well?

It's many years now
Since I wore
That lovely wedding gown,
But how I wish a magic wand
Would weave a subtle spell
And wave away my iron-grey hair

And the inches round my girth.
Cos I no longer fit into it,
Alas!

Now it's just an heirloom,
But one thing is for sure:
I've still got my original bridegroom
Of seventy years and four.

Dead Leaves

Now is the time for the counting of the
Dead leaves falling
From the tree of my youth,
When I ran my heedless run down the
Sun-kissed valley,
Crushing the sweet flowers uncaring
And trod the broad highway in hob-nail boots,
Regardless, blindly.

When pink-cheeked apple blossom tantalised
The scampering breeze and snow-soft lambs
Bleated away time's precious hours.

And I laughed and skipped and jumped and sang
In the March-torn wind, blowing the last
Dead leaves of winter,
Swirling and whirling in the distance.

And I was seventeen in my time
And the years flew like thistledown from
Dandelion meadow clocks.

But suddenly the cloud-scudding sky
Rained hailstones mingling with my salt tears,
As I lingered by the stile of my long-lost youth.

January Joy

Twelfth Night has passed
And Christmas decs
Stowed safely in the loft.

Now January, drear,
Damp, dull, is here,
Heralding in another year.

Trees drip dank
On drenched flowerbeds,
And sullen skies lour overhead.

But see there in that
Sheltered niche
A miracle appears –
A clump of golden crocus, rich,
Gladdens the gloomy, wintry day,
Proclaiming spring is on the way.

Kingfisher

A lightning flash
as a wisp of silk
shot silk
turquoise and gold
skimmed riverwards
and
vanished.

The Scream (I)

My dear, she's a scream,
A most frightful scream.
Why, they call her The Scream
Since she dished up white mice
From a pink soup tureen
To her guests.
What a scream!

She keeps a pet parrot
And takes it to market,
Perched on her shoulder.
My word, you should hear it
Cursing stallholders
In language most vulgar;
Quite a scream!

She dresses in mustard, bright blue and in
　　scarlet –
The parrot is mustard, bright blue, also scarlet.
I say, what a dream,
An absolute scream!

When crossing the street
To her it's no feat,
While trundling her trolley
She'll brandish her brolly
To halt all the traffic.
They say she's a maniac,

I think she's a scream,
A hilarious scream!

It's said that at night
When the moon, it is bright,
In her garden she prances,
Capers and dances,
Quite in the nude,
She's dreadfully rude,
The Scream, the incredible Scream!

Wearing a pair of tartan trews
She rides a bike painted red, white and blue,
Wibbly-wobbling down the street,
Waving to everyone she meets:
'Good morning, dear, and how are you?
I'm the silly old Scream from Number Two.
They call me The Scream;
I'm a scream, a regular scream!'

She's six ginger cats –
Well, just fancy that.
Wheels them into the park
Just for a lark in a Silver Cross pram,
Then feeds them on Spam
And pieces of ham
And lots of plump sprats.
Small wonder they're fat,
Those six ginger cats
Who belong to the Scream,
That crazy old dame
Who is potty and dotty and scatty and batty,
The lady they nickname The Scream.

My Bird Table

There's a very cheeky blackbird
Who appears most every day –
He perches on the feeder
And if there's nothing there,
He stares into my window,
Fixing me with beady eyes
As if to say, 'Come on, come on,
Where is my bit of bread today?'

He really is precocious
And frightens other birds away;
He even looks ferocious
Until I throw him crumbs,
Then he splashes in the bird bath
And on his way he wings.

Next comes the cocky robin,
A pert and cheerful bird,
And blue tits peck the peanuts
Suspended in wire holders,
And siskins, oh such pretty things,
And darting, tiny finches.

Later on come all the fledglings,
Blackbirds, coal tits, starlings
And fluffy little robins
Much too young to wear
Bright red vests upon their chests.

But the bonniest bird of all
Is the speckled mistle thrush –
He always comes alone,
The other birds he shuns.
So daintily he pecks the bread
And biscuit crumbs
Until the greedy pigeon swoops;
Then it's gobble, gobble, gobble.
No manners there, I do declare.
'Shoo! Shoo!' I say. 'Pray fly away,
Although I like your bill and coo,
You are not welcome here today.'

All spring and summer long
The birdsong fills me with such pleasure
And if I ever go to heaven
I hope that there will be
A little bit of woodland
Where lots and lots of songbirds
Will be there to welcome me.

Single Beds

Many years we've slept together
In our six-foot double bed,
But felt it really was high time
We vacated the nuptial couch,
So recently invested in
Two single, adjustable beds.

I can zoom my head up or my feet
With a flick of the control –
Quite independently of Hubbs –
And cuddle down into its depths
Just like a little mole.

I must admit it's rather nice
To have the bed all to myself,
For husband was inclined to twitch
And thrash his legs about.

And often he accused me
Of snatching the duvet
And, what is more, at times
He swore I'd pushed him to the floor.

The only problem is that now
I cannot stop his snoring,
As I'm not close enough
To poke or prod or kick him.

But I've hatched a very clever plan –
The long-handled feather duster to employ
To reach across the space between
And whack him firmly on the chin –
A most effective ploy.

But since we've gone our separate ways
I truly must admit,
I rather miss the warmth of him
When nights are raw and chill
And find the need to take a
Rubber bottle to my celibate crib,
Though it's not the same as cuddling up
In the matrimonial bed!

Blue for a Boy

'Dear God, not again!' Meg could barely utter the words for shock as, taking the telephone over to a chair, she sat down heavily. 'Are you quite sure, Sally? You're not pulling my leg, are you?'

On the other end of the phone, Sally gave a happy chuckle. 'No, Mummy, it's quite definite and I'm nearly five months. The baby is due in September.'

'But, Sally, isn't it rather risky? You'll be forty-three next month. Is it wise to have gone in for another baby at your age? There could be problems, dear.'

'Oh no, Mumsie, everything is fine. I've had tests and a scan and you won't believe it, but they tell me it's a boy this time. Isn't it just too wonderful?'

'Oh Sally, I am so very pleased for you and Richard must be delighted.'

'Of course he is, especially after my presenting him with four daughters. It came as a bit of a surprise, I can tell you and...'

Meg interrupted her. 'But I can't help feeling that it's a bit irresponsible, Sally, dear. I thought you'd decided not to have any more family. Surely you didn't plan this baby.'

'Well, Mum, the truth is that I got a bit careless over the Christmas period and, well, it is a time of good will to men, isn't it?'

Meg could hear the laughter in Sally's voice. 'Sally, dear, that's not nice.' She never ceased to marvel at her youngest daughter, who went through life as though it was all one big joke. If she encountered a problem, she ignored it and invariably it went away or was solved for her by other people. Her home always seemed to be in a state of chaos, her excuse being that she was organised in a very disorganised manner. She was so unlike Jane, the eldest of her two daughters, who was rather prim and house-proud. Meg never ceased to wonder how she had managed to produce two offspring with such different characters.

Whatever would Jane say when she heard the news? How often had she reprimanded Sally for breeding so prolifically, pointing out the threat of a population explosion? Jane had managed to limit her family to one child. Dearly as Meg loved dear Jane, she sometimes wished she was not quite so pompous.

'Are you still there, Mummy?'

Sally's voice brought her out of the reverie. 'Oh sorry, dear, I'm still listening, but…'

'The thing is, Mumsie,' Sally went on without waiting for Meg to continue, 'we didn't plan for this baby, never thought about it in our wildest dreams and, in a way, it's rather rocked the boat, or should I say the cradle?' she added with a giggle. 'As you know, we've got quite a large bank loan to pay off which we took out last autumn to pay for the garden to be landscaped, the new conservatory and fitted kitchen. Ritchie's salary is very good and, with my part-time job, we manage OK, but you do see we have a bit of a problem, that is, if I give up work.'

Dear God, not again, thought Meg. So that Sally could go to work, Meg had looked after all four of her children for a few hours each day until they were of school age, besides babysitting on numerous occasions. The last child had commenced school the previous term and Meg was enjoying her new-found freedom. She and Tom had been able to go out a lot more together and she did not get so tired these days either.

'So you see, Mum,' Sally continued, 'Ritchie and I wondered if you could possibly take over the baby when I return to work. It wouldn't be for too long, Mummy dear, I promise, and I'm sure I could cut down my hours a bit. It would only be for a few more months, well, maybe a year…or so, just until the loan is paid off.'

Meg sighed. She had always found it impossible to say 'No' to Sally, but this time she held back.

'I'll have to think about it, dear, and there's Dad to consider. I've a feeling he won't be all that co-operative this time. You must realise that we shall, neither of us, see seventy again and one does tend to get tired now.'

'Oh rubbish, Mummy. I never cease to marvel at your stamina. You're so energetic and just wonderful with children. The problem is that if I do have to hand in my notice, I must inform my employer as soon as possible so that someone else can be trained to take over my job. I'll ring you on Saturday after you've had a chat about it with Dad and, of course, we'll quite understand if you feel you can't oblige.

'Don't worry about it, Mummy dear. Must dash. Love to Dad.'

'All right, Sally, take care, darling.' As Meg replaced the telephone, she heard Sally humming a gay tune. There she goes again, thought Meg. Offloading her problem on to someone else in her subtle way.

At that moment, Tom, her husband, came in from the garden and Meg busied herself making a pot of tea. She waited until he sat down, then fired her bombshell.

'Sally rang just now. She had some news.'

'Everything's all right over there, isn't it?' Tom sounded alarmed. 'Is one of the children ill?'

'No, no, Tom, they're fine, but I don't think you're going to believe this. Sally is having another baby, due in September, and they tell her it will be a boy.'

'Well, bless me, that's a big surprise. At her age too. Never thought she'd have any more after the four girls. She's OK, isn't she? No problems? Best bit of news I've heard for a long time. You know I've always wanted a boy in the family, but aren't they a bit irresponsible, Meg? After all, with all these contraptions these days…'

'You mean contraceptives, dear,' Meg corrected him. 'They didn't plan this baby. It seems that Sally got a bit careless over the Christmas period. Know what she said, Tom? That Christmas was a season of goodwill to men, the naughty girl.'

Tom chuckled. 'Just the sort of excuse she would think up. Oh well, she'll have to give up her job this time.'

'Well, Tom, there is a snag. You see, she would like us to look after the babe for a while, just until they get the bank loan paid off, which they took out for all that work they had done last autumn.' Meg paused as she saw the expression on Tom's face. He was an easygoing man and she would usually have no difficulty in manipulating him but, at times, he could surprise her by taking a very firm stand.

'Sally has got a nerve, and that husband of hers. Haven't you done enough looking after all her brood so that she could go to work? We're just beginning to enjoy our old age now that her youngest started school last term. Of course you told her it was out of the question. You gave her a definite "no", didn't you?'

'Well, Tom, I said we would talk it over. She wants to know by Saturday so that if she has to leave her job, they can get another person in straight away to train for her particular work.'

Tom nearly exploded with anger. 'She's gone too far this time. It's all your fault. You've spoilt her, Meg. You can just get on the phone and say there's nothing to talk about. Remind her we're retired and while we don't mind doing the odd bit of babysitting, you're not playing nanny to her fifth. That's final. I don't want to hear another word on the matter. The subject is closed.' And Tom stomped out of the lounge and into the garden, where Meg saw him furiously hacking away at something in the shrub border.

Pouring herself out another cup of tea, she lay back and began daydreaming, visualising yet another baby in the old pram under the pear tree, thinking of the exquisite sensation she always experienced when cradling the tiny body in her arms. They still had all the baby things in the loft: the battered playpen, the high chair and the pink cot she had used for her own girls and Sally's. The latter would need repainting and… From daydreaming, she slipped into a happy doze, not stirring until Tom reappeared, his garden jobs now completed and needing a meal.

'You see, Meg,' he commented. 'Shows you must be feeling your age sleeping in the afternoon. Never used to do that, so how the devil do you think you could take on yet another of Sally's babies? Have you rung her?'

'I'll do it later, Tom, I promise.' Meg disappeared into the kitchen.

Several days passed and neither Tom nor Meg referred to the subject which was uppermost in their minds.

The day before Sally was to ring, Meg went off to her weekly meeting. She had recently joined a club in the village and enjoyed mixing with people of her own age.

On returning, she walked round to the back garden to let Tom know she was back. He was nowhere to be seen but, noticing the shed door open and thinking he was inside, she called to him. There was no answer. She peeped inside. He was not there but, propped up against his bench, was the old pink cot and nearby a pot of paint. Picking it up, she looked at the label on the tin. 'Duck-egg blue' it read.

Witch in the Cottage

When I am very, very old,
I'll live alone in an ancient cottage, thatched.
Keep a few hens to scratch
And scrabble in the yard,
Some bees, a jet-black cat.
Bake my own bread
And wear upon my head
A red sunbonnet.
Buy cuckoo clocks,
Grow marigolds,
Sweet herbs and hollyhocks –
Shan't worry about weeds.
Wear faded frocks.
I won't dress up for callers;
Might not wash,
Depending on my mood.
Some days I'll sit and brood
For hours and hours.
Eat what and when I like,
Bend all the rules,
Who cares?
I'll swear and swear,
No one to hear.
Weave a few spells;
They'll call me a witch,
The witch in the cottage.
Can't wait until I'm really old
Instead of only eight.

Three Gulf War Poems

1. He is My Brother

He is my brother, this Iraqi solder,
Lying spread-eagled, bleeding in the sand,
And I can only say to him that I am sorry
And I can only take him by the hand.
I had my orders, could not disobey, mate;
I bear no malice, you I do not hate,
But your dictator is a fiendish tyrant
Who overran the country of Kuwait;
And now has set ablaze its oil wells,
And made of desert skies a smoke-filled hell.

We shall not rest until he is defeated
And peace out here is once again restored.

Yet even as I speak, your lifeblood's draining,
Staining the sand until each grain turns crimson
—
Why then do I feel shame?

Because, Iraqi soldier, you're my brother,
And as I watch you die, I say a prayer:
Dear Lord, no, never, ever,
Will nations need to fight another war.

2. The Aftermath

In the mountain pass,
In the wilderness
Where nothing grows,
Through the ice and snow,
A woman cries,
A small child dies,
A multitude,
Refugees,
The dregs of war.
It's all happened before.

Who can we turn to?
They cry to the sky.
Help us, oh help us
Before we all die.

Great armies came with fierce weapons of war
And pushed back the tyrant from Kuwait's
    door,
But the job was unfinished,
They failed to dislodge
The monster
So we had a go,
But he was still strong,
A formidable foe
Who murders and maims.
Tell us, what was the gain?

Freedom for some
But hell for so many.
Cities impoverished,
Gulf waters polluted,
Oil wells afire,
Our heritage ruined.
Was there no other way?

Where shall we go?
How shall we live?
We're unwanted,
A rag-tag of war.
It's all happened before.

3. Thanksgiving

Why are we here
Praying to God?
To fight was their job,
And they had the weapons most deadly
To push back the fiend.

Casualties minimal.
'Now thank we all our God,'
Though the desert and cities
Ran red
With
Blood
Of young men and old,
Boys and girls,
Women with child.

Thank you, God, for the mess that is left,
The heartache, the tears,
The starving, the pain,
The suckling babe
Killed by a missile.

The organ booms, the bells ring out.
'Now thank we all our God,'
The congregation shout,
Well-heeled and full-bellied,
Forgotten by some
The plight of the many,
Homeless, legless and fearful,
Facing the scourge

Stalking the land,
The thousands still fleeing
The barbaric hand
Of their leader.

Why are we here?

Year's End

It is over,
Finished,
The glow has vanished
And the wind blows shrill,
Tearing the sere leaves
From branches
Till trees
Stand
Naked.

Summer has long since gathered her skirts
And left autumn to limp into bleak winter.

Pert robin's penny whistle
Penetrates dark, misty mornings
And rowan berries fade, shrivelling.

Gossamer webs hang shrouding hedges,
Grey and glistening;
Sunflowers droop heavy heads, blackened
And brown seeded
And conkers thud unheeded
In dripping
Woods.

All is drear,
Finished,
Extinguished.

But bear with patience winter's frigid grip,
For, in a while, borne on a warm, west wind,
Sweet spring will smile.

The Red Dwarf

(Portrait of a Chief Inspector)

Superintendent Grumbellow was not a happy man. It was Monday morning and raining. His in-tray was overflowing and, worst of all, he was expecting a new chief inspector on his staff to replace Sydney Solvitall who had just retired. He sighed as he pulled his in-tray towards him. Suddenly his office door flew open, preceded by a thunderous rapping. A strange apparition stood before him. 'Chief Inspector René Apprehendor reporting, sir,' the apparition announced in a staccato voice.

Good God, he thought, they had not informed me that my new chief was a woman – and what a sight. As Apprehendor advanced towards him, his analytical eye registered every detail. Height approximately four feet ten inches, age fifty plus, stocky, box-like build, outsize feet – size nine, if he was not mistaken. Frizzy, greying hair sticking out under a bright red hat with a pink feather. Short black suit, cheeks brightly rouged, lipstick smudged and, as she grinned at him, her large discoloured teeth put him in mind of the race horse Red Rum.

'They called me the Red Dwarf at my last station,' she chortled, holding out a podgy hand, which gripped his with such force that he all but fell forward into his in-tray.

For once, Grumbellow was at a loss for words. 'Send in Loafer,' he called urgently through his intercom. A few seconds later, Loafer, a hefty six-footer, burst through the door. 'This is Sergeant Loafer, your assistant,' he told Apprehendor. She looked Loafer up and down, taking in the pink-cheeked youth with the baby face.

'Well, Loafer, let's get to work. There'll be no loafing around while you work with me, my man. Ha! Ha! Ha!'

Loafer's heart sank and the Superintendent sighed again.

Bluebells

Yesterday this woodland glade
Was covered deep in brown,
Autumn's residue,
But now today it is as though
The sky had fallen through
The leafy trees to form a sea
Of blue, deep purple blue.

And everywhere the overture of spring
Is tuning up,
A prelude to midsummer
As light winds gently ruffle
And through the green leaves rustle.

Woodpeckers' beaks are beating time,
Tap-tap-tap a-tapping,
And cuckoos calling sound a chorus
To pigeons endless cooing
As bumblebees go buzzing
And bluebells softly ring in
A symphony of summer.

So when dark thoughts
The mind oppress
As winter drear draws near,
Remember scenes of summer
When the sky fell through

The leafy trees
And made a sea of blue,
Rich purple blue.

And, if you listen carefully,
You might just hear an echo
Of cuckoos still 'a-cucking'
And bluebells ring-a-ringing.

The Night-wind Fairies (II)

Last night I tossed and tossed and turned,
Sleep declined to be my guest,
When above the white owl's hooting
I heard the sound of laughing
Like tiny bells a-tinkling.

I tiptoed to the casement
And there to my surprise
I saw the night-wind fairies
Streaming through the skies,
Flying up the moonbeams
Like twinkling, shimmering stars.

Their gowns were made of gossamer,
Their wings with silver lined,
Their hair as gold as ripening corn,
Flared and flashing on the wind.

They flew into my bedroom
And frolicked in my hair,
Then took my hands and flew with me
Out through the balmy air.

They fluttered to the garden,
Plucking the pretty flowers
And wove a wreath of petals
Into my long fair hair.

We danced and danced the hours away,
Twirling, whirling, circling,
Like fireflies darting, sparkling.

But when the moon its course had run
And dawn lit up the east,
The night-wind fairies flew away
Before the rising sun.

Next morning when I wakened,
I could scarce believe my eyes.
For there beside my pillow
Lay a wreath of fragrant flowers,
Glistening with dew drops
Like pearls among the petals.

Then I heard a tiny echo
Of little bells a-tinkling
And I knew I'd not been dreaming.

Mum

(In Memoriam)

She lay so still,
Her silver hair
framing
Her tired face.
Her work-worn hands
On the coverlet
Unmoving.

But, as I gazed,
I saw her young again,
A child,
Chasing a ball,
Playing with dolls,
Clasping teddy,
Chubby hands
Clutching the fur,

Toddling,
Fingers embracing,
Clinging to Mum's neck,
Kissing.

Later, learning her letters,
Pencil poised,
Scribbling,
Colouring,
Lips pursed.

Rolling hoops,
Playing hopscotch.

Leaving school,
Making her way
In the work-a-day world,
Earning a wage,
A few pounds a year
In domestic service,
Rising in time
As head of the kitchen,
Cooking.

Those hands always labouring,
Rarely at rest.

In the fullness of time
Marriage
And a home of her own,
Then children
And the endless round of
Cooking,

Washing,
Cleaning,
Shopping,
Mending,
Ironing.
No mod cons;
Making ends meet –
The once chubby hands
Reddening,
Wrinkling,
Seldom resting.

Wiping away tears,
Bandaging hurts,
Always ready to listen.

Reading stories at bedtime,
Saying prayers –
'Gentle Jesus meek and mild'.
Training and teaching,
Giving herself constantly
In the service of others.
Smoothing the path.

Wise and intelligent,
Clever at crosswords,
Making time for her reading,
Mothers' Union and
Church Sunday mornings.

Coping when war came
With rationing

And fears for her loved ones,
Then losing a son –
Life can be cruel.
Those hands still as busy
Keeping things normal,
Hiding the heartache.
Always there for her family
And loyal to her husband,
Loving and caring,
Growing old gracefully.

Now the raven-black hair
Turned to silver,
The hands lined and tired,
All tasks at an end –
Those hands so industrious,
composed,
quiescent,
resting
AT
PEACE.

Blackcurrant Jam for Our Tea

Blackcurrant jam
For tea
Smelling of summer,
High summer,
Though outside the house
Winds howl,
Battering bare, leafless trees.

Rain patters unceasingly,
A dark, December day,
But in my heart
It is July
And skies are blue
As periwinkles
And insects dart,
Hovering,
Humming
Above blackcurrant bushes,
The sun-soaked fruit
Hanging heavy in clusters,
Like polished beads
Under meshes of
Summer's green leaves.

Picker's fingers staining
Purple,
Planning wine- and jam- and jelly-making,

Rich, dark ruby gems;
Nature's bounty
To be plundered and stored
In glass jam jars and bottles.

★

Alas, summer's vision is vanished
And the rain still is pouring
And the wind still is howling,
But to me it's July,
High summer
And skies are blue as periwinkles,
Cos there's blackcurrant jam for our tea.

Not a Good Day

I should have stayed in bed
On Friday, 25th of Feb,
But how was I to know
Exactly how the day would go
And by the time it ended
I'd be quite demented?

It all began at seven
When our milkman (he's from Devon)
Rushed the garden gate
In such a hurry, couldn't wait,
But it was jammed, and sailing over
Landed in a patch of clover –
Broke his leg, poor blighter.

Then the baby's milk boiled over,
And our dog, his name is Rover,
Threw up on the bedroom carpet,
So I mopped it up with Harpic.

After that, went off to market,
But our car, there is no doubt,
Is well and truly quite clapped out.
Had to catch the bus, took buggy,
But forgot the poor old baby.

Back I went, but realised
I'd left the front door key inside,
So climbed up ladder to bathroom window,
But in house I could not go,
My rear end being much too big,
Cos for cream cakes I'm a pig.

I was well and truly stuck
Until there came a stroke of luck
When window cleaner rescued me
And, after several cups of tea,
Congratulated me on my taste in underwear.
Said he'd never seen a pair
Of prettier, frillier knickers.

As I left for bus once more,
A lady knocked on my front door
And placing a foot inside the hall
Said on me she'd come to call
To say the world would end next week
And was I ready my Maker to meet?
I slammed the door and heard her shriek,
'Remember I warned you the world ends next
    week.'
So I shouted, 'Sod off, woman, you're up the
    creek.'

Exhausted from market, I reached home
To find on the doorstep Aunty Joan,
Uncle Jack and Great Aunt Maude,
Sam and Dan, Phillip and Claude,
And by the time they'd all been fed
All I wanted was my bed.

I waved them off at half past six
As husband appeared, so I had to fix
Him a meal, but tripped over the bloody cat,
Who leapt on the table and made off with the
    chop
And when husband slunk off to the Kettle
And Pot,
I dumped the baby into his cot.

I'd had enough, I'd had my lot –
To bed I went with a double, double scotch,
An erotic book and a box of chocs.
To hell with the darning and all the ironing.
I pulled down the blind on Feb 25th,
Hoping for better things on Feb 26th.

The Last Supper

Esther had mentioned the fact so many times over the past twenty years or so that she almost believed it would really happen. 'I shall be satisfied to live until I'm eighty if I'm in good health, but I have no desire to go on until I get to the stage when I have to be put into a home for the elderly,' she would tell her friends. She had rather hoped for a swift death at that age, but today was her eightieth birthday and her health, so the doctor assured her, was excellent. It hardly looked as though she was going to make a rapid exit.

Life had been sweet until a few months ago, but today she was full of bitterness. Having always enjoyed a loving relationship with her only child, Ruthie, and her son-in-law, it seemed for some reason they were now neglecting her. Oh, there were the phone calls, but every time she mentioned a visit, they had been evasive – always some excuse. Richard was tied up with work, a conference, or they had friends staying, or Ruthie was working extra hours. Esther fully understood they lived busy lives, both having exacting jobs, but surely they could at least spare a weekend to come to see her, or even invite her to stay with them?

She had long ago given up any thought of a grandchild. Ruthie, now in her forty-second year, was a confirmed career woman so was hardly likely to oblige. Then there had been talk of Richard putting in for a transfer so that they could be nearer, but nothing had come of it.

Now Esther was going to make her stock phrase come true. She was going to leave the world today. It was obvious now she was ageing, she was not wanted. She was becoming a liability.

This evening she would prepare her last supper. Take some tablets after the meal with some wine. Having been in the nursing profession, she knew just what to do. The sleeping tablets were ready on a small table by the sofa. Her doctor had been very reluctant to prescribe them, but she had managed to convince him that she was having disturbed nights and he had given in to her request.

The day wore on. I ought to feel different, she told herself. Apprehensive, certainly guilty or even excited, but she felt quite ordinary, just like any other day. If only Ruthie had remembered her birthday, but there had been nothing. No card, letter or phone call. It was so out of character.

Old Sam next door would find her in the morning when he made his usual daily call to see if she was all right. A pang of regret, even remorse, swept over her. Dear Sam, such a good neighbour. His vegetable patch kept her supplied with produce all year round. He would miss her too, as well as the tasty dishes she handed him over the fence from time to time.

Her last supper had been chosen carefully. Smoked salmon with a crisp green salad and crusty bread with a bottle of three-year old Cabernet Sauvignon, which was chilling in the fridge. Lemon sorbet to follow. She would put the pansy cloth on the table. Tom had always liked it. He had died five years ago. How horrified he would be if he knew what she was about to do, but my life's my own, she told herself. Surely I can do what I like with it.

The chiming clock struck six. Time to eat, then she would do what was necessary. Elgar's *Enigma Variations* would be rather nice to go out to. She inserted the tape into the cassette player.

She was about to fetch the salmon and salad from the fridge, when the phone rang. 'Damn,' she said, exasperated. 'Probably Betty Marcheson ringing about the WI committee meeting next week and she'll go on as usual.'

'Hello,' she said, rather irritably.

'Hello, Mum.' It was Richard.

'Hello, Richard,' she answered coldly.

'Mum, I'm so sorry about your birthday card, but I've just found it in my jacket pocket. Ruthie asked me to post it, but I clean forgot. You see things have been a bit topsy-turvy here lately.' He sounded very excited. 'You see, Mum, I've got a big surprise for you. Are you sitting down?'

Whatever was the man on about, Esther wondered. 'Yes, I'm sitting on the sofa, Richard.'

'Well, first of all, Mum, we want to apologise and explain why it's been so long since we've seen you, but you will be surprised to hear that Ruthie was pregnant when you last saw her, three months actually, and because there have been complications, her being nearly forty-two and it being her first, she absolutely refused to let me tell you, knowing how you would worry. I was all for putting you in the picture, but she was adamant. Anyway, everything's fine and she gave birth to a daughter about two hours ago. No problems at all. A straightforward birth.'

Esther had been silent while Richard was speaking, too stunned by the news to utter a word.

'Mum, are you still there?' Richard asked.

'But, Richard, are you saying that Ruthie has had a baby? I just can't believe it. I can't believe it.'

'Well, it's true and Ruthie wants to call her Esther after you. We knew you'd like that. And, Mum, some more news. I've got my transfer to your area so we'll be seeing a lot more of you, and Ruthie is so thrilled. She wants the baby to really get to know her grandma.'

'Oh Richard, are you quite sure everything is all right? I can hardly take it in.' Esther began to cry.

'Yes, of course, they're both fine and Ruthie sends her very best love. I'll ring tomorrow. Right now, I must phone some other people, but we wanted you to be the first to know.'

Esther replaced the phone, but did not move. The news seemed to have robbed her of movement. A baby in the family after all these years and she a grandma; and on top of that, they were coming to live nearby. Shock gave way to excitement and she almost ran into the garden. She must tell Sam.

'Sam, Sam, where are you? Quick, come here,' she called.

'Anything wrong, Esther?' he asked, popping his weather-beaten face over the hedge. 'Whatever is the matter?'

'You'll never guess, Sam, but there's a baby and they are coming to live down here and everything's all right.

It's wonderful, wonderful.' Esther picked up the corner of her apron and began crying again.

'Steady on, Esther.' Sam was mystified. 'What baby and who are you talking about?'

'I'm so excited,' Esther answered between sobs. 'Why don't you come in and have supper with me, then I'll explain?'

'That would be nice, Esther. Give me a few minutes to get washed up and changed.' And he hurried off, whistling. He had been rather concerned about her lately. He knew she had been upset at not seeing that daughter of hers for some time and, when he had wished her a happy birthday earlier, she had been unusually preoccupied. She's up to something, he had thought.

And then there were the tablets she had asked him to collect for her from the chemist. She was not one for taking sleeping tablets. No, he had felt concerned and had decided to look in on her later to reassure himself that all was well. Thank goodness she seemed happy enough right now, so maybe he had been worrying unduly.

Meanwhile, Esther laid another place at the table, then fetched the food and wine from the fridge, opening the latter to let it breathe a bit. She began to sing a nursery rhyme – 'Wee Willie Winkie runs through the town'. How did it go? She must look out Ruthie's old book and refresh her memory.

She replaced Elgar's *Enigma Variations* with a Vera Lyn record. 'It's a lovely day tomorrow,' Vera Lyn sang. 'Tomorrow is a lovely day.'

A knock at the door and Sam was calling, 'Can I come in?' His face, cleanly scrubbed, shone under his freshly brushed hair, which stood up round his head like a white, woolly halo. In his hands he held a bunch of lilies of the valley. 'The first this year,' he told her as he put then into her hands. 'Now, what is all this about a baby, eh?'

Esther gave him the news. 'Oh Sam, isn't life just wonderful?' Once again the tears fell.

'There, there. Well, I'll be blowed.' He patted her on the shoulder. 'I'll have to put in a few more rows of tatties and beans if the little family are coming down here.'

'You're so good, Sam,' she gulped between sobs. 'Now come and sit here, opposite me.' He sat down, bowed his head and then, folding his hands together, said grace. It was then, out of the corner of his eye, he saw the bottle of tablets on the table by the sofa. He'd been right to worry, he thought.

Esther helped him to a portion of fish, then took the bread and broke it, handing him a piece. She poured the wine into two goblets, passing one to him. He raised it to his lips, looking her straight in the eye. 'Reminds you of the Last Supper,' he remarked.

'Yes, you could say that, Sam,' she answered, glancing at her plate, not daring to look him straight in the eye.

I Remember

Most days I can't remember
One minute from the next –
Where I left my knitting, my handbag
or my specs.
I leave umbrellas in the shops,
My purse on countertops,
Often mislay shopping lists
And even walking sticks.
Cogitate on names and dates –
I'm just a silly old thing.

Yet very strange to me it seems
That always in the spring,
The sweet scent of azaleas
Drenched in May moonbeams
Unlocks a precious memory,
When I recall so vividly
Your laughing eyes, your dear, young face,
Relive again our close embrace.

Why does the scent of azaleas
Haunt me down the years,
Stirring up old memories
That fill my eyes with tears?

Seasons

When cherry blossom stains blue skies
And cuckoos call from tree to tree,
When round the eaves the swallows dive
And blackbird sings so cheerily,
And later when the dragonfly
Skims and shimmers on the lake
And waxen water lilies wake
And fleecy lambs frisk, gambolling,
Then sings my heart a song of Spring
And listens to the bluebells sing.

When Summer sun unlocks the rose
And slim laburnum drips its gold,
When plundering bee impregnates flowers
And buttercups bejewel the fields,
When honeysuckle scents the air
And giant sunflower petals flare
And balmy breezes, soft and sweet,
Rustle through the golden wheat,
Then sings my heart a hymn of praise
For glorious, glowing, sunny days.

When early frosts the leaves encrust
And Autumn paints in rouge and rust,
And spangled spider webs adorn
The hedges, bushes and the lawn,
Sparkling and gleaming in the sun,

And hips and haws splash brilliant hue
Like blood-red scars all wet with dew
And gorse pods crack and split and spew,
Then sings my heart a thankful prayer
For riches fair beyond compare.

When Winter lays the land threadbare
And icy winds rip through the trees,
Wailing and moaning in despair
Like thunderous waves on heaving seas,
When earth lies brittle, hard and cold
And sullen sun hoards up her gold,
A fragile flower defies the snow
And on my heart it casts a glow,
A harbinger of gladsome Spring,
Then I a joyful anthem sing.

Man of Straw

'What is a man who is no more than everything
    he owns
Yet one day loses everything he owns?'[1]

He is nothing –
An empty shell without a soul,
Without an anchor in adversity,
For when storm clouds gather
He is tossed up on the flood,
A piece of flotsam,
A drowning man clutching at straws,
For he knows nothing of love, compassion or
    charity,
Possessing no inner strength to sustain him
In the face of calamity.
He may call for help, but no one is there
To comfort him.
Yet if, as the currents take him,
And he sinks deeper and deeper into an abyss of
    misery,
He prays to his God for deliverance
And asks for forgiveness for his selfish life,
Then a spark may be kindled in his heart
And his soul fly back to his bruised body
And he will be made truly whole again;
And though he loses all he owns,
He will have gained the world.

---

[1] Source of first two lines unknown.

The Deserted Beach

An eyelash of a moon gazes down on the empty beach, no longer peopled by day-trippers and holidaymakers. Yesterday is spent, tomorrow is out of sight and only tonight hovers over many turreted sandcastles, displaying bravely waving pennants and dried-up moats.

Waves softly hiss and swish as the incoming tide gradually engulfs toppling castles, rippling and smoothing the sand.

A child's pink, plastic shoe bobs to and fro in the water and a small crab scuttles lopsidedly from a many-mussled rock pool.

A sprinkling of gulls rides the waves, satiated after greedily guzzling titbits scattered by benevolent tourists.

A gentle breeze blows, bearing echoes of yesterday's voices:

'Come and see my sandcastle, Mum,' and, 'Let's bury Dad in the sand.'

A wooden spade is washed out to sea and a many-coloured beach ball is thrown up onto the sand.

Odours linger from closed and shuttered fish and chip shops and takeaways, blending with salt and seaweed smells.

Baited lobster pots out at sea wait to entrap unsuspecting victims.

The beach is washed clean as the tide creeps in, slurping and slopping against slippery breakwaters.

Sun-dried limpets squelch and gurgle as water cascades over their rocky beds.

An eyelash of a moon looks down on the deserted beach. It is tonight. Tomorrow is out of sight.

A Cornfield Has Two Faces

High summer and skylarks warbling,
Making sweet music
Under cloudless, blue skies
Above sunflower-yellow corn
And poppy petals, tissue paper thin,
Rustling and trembling.

Bees buzzing, fussing
Among wild flowers
And grasshoppers' incessant rasping
And myriad insects strumming,
Nature's orchestra,
A medley of summer harmony… Peace.

But suddenly it seemed to me
That storm clouds hovered, menacing,
Blotting out the sun
And distant thunder rumbled
As lightning flashed and flickered.

Stiff breezes charged through brittle corn
And hailstones flew
Like fusillades
Battering fragile poppies,
Staining the field blood red,
And my heart bled
For Flanders,
Remembering.

Then I heard the din and crackle
Of long gone war-torn battle,
Saw lacerated skin,
The bloody bandaged limb,
The screaming, dying men.
Smelt stinking stench
Of muddied trench,
Heard whine of shot and crump of shell,
Machine-guns muttering, stuttering
In that ghastly, murdering hell.

But above the battle's discord,
A lark began to sing
As the din and roar receded.
Bees still went buzz, buzz buzzing
And crickets rasping, rasping
Under poppy flowers swaying
To the summer zephyrs teasing.

Peace was in the cornfield,
But my heart still bleeds
For Flanders,
Remembering.

Lament for a Dead Twin

Two tiny seeds
In the womb of our mother,
Bonding together
Long before birth,
You and I,
Darling twin brother.

Sharing the cot,
The pram and our toys,
Gurgling and kicking
And making a noise.

Remember dear old Donk?
We took him to school
When we started at five,
A strange looking creature,
A sort of a mule.
'No, no,' Teacher said,

'No mules are allowed
To attend this school.
That is our rule.'

I nicknamed you Dogger,
Dearest twin brother.

Such fun and games
All our childhood days,
Carefree and gay,
Our world so secure.

Confirmed together
By the Bishop of Rochester,
I in my white dress,
You in your surplice.

What a tease you were,
A wonderful wit,
Yet caring and kind.

You chaperoned me
At our very first ball
And dared me to flirt
Or make dates with strange boys –
Remember!

But at twenty years old
You suddenly died…
How I cried and cried.

Yet sometimes I feel
You are not far away,

The bond is unbroken
Though you went away.

And now I am aged,
My hair turning grey,
I still miss you, Dogger,
My darling twin brother.

The Innocents

Then Herod, when he saw that he was mocked of the Wise Men, was exceeding wroth, and sent forth and slew all the children that were in Bethlehem, and in all the coasts thereof, from two years old and under, according to the time which he had diligently inquired of the Wise Men.

St Matthew 2:16

Was the devil abroad
At the time King Herod
Ordered the killings
Of the innocent babies
In Bethlehem and beyond?

Were the Wise Men to blame
When they made their claim
That a King had been born
When they followed the star?

Or was Herod so furious
To think he'd a rival,
So bade his soldiers
Slay innocent babies,
Hoping to eliminate Jesus?

So where was God
Who His Son had sent
To redeem us,

But ensured Jesus fled
With Mary and Joseph,
Yet left for dead
All those innocent babies?

Oh, the wailing and weeping
And great lamentations
From the mothers in mourning.

Where were You, God? Where were You?

Creation versus Evolution

Philip Henry Gosse 1810–1888
Was the Attenborough of his day,
Writing books on plants and animals
To educate the people.

And Philip Henry Gosse 1810–1888
Was the man who said
God put fossils in the rocks
To deceive geologists,
But was a laughing stock of popular science,
Maintaining that Adam, not being born of
    woman,
Required no remnant of his non-existent
    umbilical cord…

But then like a clap of thunder
Charles Darwin tore asunder Gosse's hunches,
Expounding all his theories
On the origin of the species.

★

Creation
            or
                    evolution:
Was Gosse right or Darwin wrong?

The scientists can speculate
And disseminate hypotheses,
But one thing is for certain,
A global deracination
Would end the speculation
Of
      evolution
                    or
                             creation,
Resulting in extinction
And abrogate this knotty question.

My Favourite Season

I love springtime the very best,
When sweet birds sing
And blackbirds nest
High up in the hawthorn hedge
And April's tears
Bestir the glossy celandine
And cuckoos call and daffodils
Dance in the wind and loudly shrill,
Prompting the perfumed, passive rose
Its crimson petals to disclose.

When soft winds stroke the cherry buds,
Their frothy blossom to unlock,
And sunshine's golden tongue persuades
A butterfly to flit and flirt
Among the early fragrant flowers –
Oh how I love the springtime hours.

But then when summer's fiery breath
Frolics with the gaudy blooms
And sets alight the yellow broom,
And honeysuckle, rose and lily
Scent the air and merrily
The larks do sing
And busy building swallows
Glide and dive around the eaves,
And green-leaved trees

Wear summer vests –
The stately sunflower,
A late guest,
All clothed in gold,
Bronze-seeded chest.
Perhaps I like the summer best.

But then there's autumn
When I see the whirling,
Red and golden leaves.
The waving corn all golden hued
And heathered moor in purple robe,
When summer's gate is slammed tight up
Shuttered and cobwebbed, all bedewed,
And robins pipe a mournful whistle
And sport a bonny, blushing breast.

And what of winter
When winds shriek
And rime paints trees
And all is dismal, dank and bleak,
When snug indoors in cosy nook,
Curled up with a favourite book,
No lawns to mow,
No seeds to sow,
No weeding, watering, cultivating,
And in the larder many jars
Of home-made jam
And russet apples, ripe and sweet.

But in my tiny cut glass vase
A late rose blooms and seems to say

Nature sleeps, but in a while,
Sweet spring will come again and smile.

Which season do I like the best?
Each one brings joy, each one brings pleasure,
A few short months for us to treasure.

The yearly cycle runs its course,
But if I had to make a choice,
For me the springtime would come first.

My Secret Place

I found a secret place one day,
A meadow wild with flowers gay,
Buttercups and poppies red,
Lady's bedstraw in the hedge –
Ragged robin, purple vetches,
Meadow-sweet and green-flowered sedges.

But wondrous fair than any there,
Growing in that grassy dell
Was the frail and dainty blue harebell,
Frilly cupped on wiry stem,
Timidly trembling in the wind.

★

But yesterday a rape took place
And I heard a dreadful sound
As gangs of men with cruel machines
Laid to waste my secret place
To build a massive car park
And a Sainsbury's supermarket.

★

So today I took a bus to town
And purchased wild flower seeds
To recreate my secret place
And plant them in my lawn,

225

Then when summer's golden, glowing sun
Awakes my sleeping seeds
And breezes softly sing,
There'll be wild flowers in profusion
Among lush, tufty grasses –
Orchids, toadflax, speedwell, daisies,
Harebells, yarrow, cowslips, cornflowers,
And I'll know my secret place is safe
From man's stupidity
And giant machine's ferocity.

My Strange Collection

Are you an inveterate collector? Do you accumulate works of art, silver spoons, thimbles, old postcards? I cannot say I ever intended joining the ranks of ardent collectors but, nevertheless, have indeed done so over the years, though, unlike many who travel far and wide, seeking rare objects and specimens to enlarge their collection, mine comes to me unwanted and unwelcome. My particular hobby is called collecting embarrassing experiences, some of which I would like to share with you.

It all began years ago, one incident being still vividly etched on my mind.

My boyfriend was home on leave. I was ecstatic. Here I was sitting on a grassy hillock while he read me a poem. A distant cuckoo called. The scents of early summer wafted on a light breeze. My cup was full.

Then it happened. At first, it was only a slight tickling sensation travelling up my right leg. I ignored it, but the tickling increased, changing in intensity to nasty little nippings. I squirmed as decorously as possible under the circumstances.

Years later I would have treated the episode as a joke; admitted I seemed to have ants in my pants and retired behind the nearest bush to attend to matters. This, however, was the early forties, and it was not considered etiquette, in my circle anyway, for a shy young maiden to mention nether garments in front of a member of the opposite sex.

I tried shifting my position, but to no avail. A small army was busy waging war all over the lower part of my anatomy.

My adorable intoned on:

> *Into our hearts high yearnings come*
> *welling and surging in.*
> *Come from the mystic regions...*

I could stand the irritation no longer. Uttering a yell, I leapt to my feet and rushed homewards. My bewildered beau gave chase, only to find my mother's amply proportioned frame blocking the doorway of my home as, with arms akimbo, she demanded to know just what he had been getting up to with her daughter. A veteran of many bombing raids over enemy territory, he was no match for her. Turning tail, he fled.

Another more recent experience of quite a different nature occurred when I was dining at a friend's home. I saw, to my delight, that a starter of mackerel pâté had been prepared. Now, I just adore this dish and my salivary glands went straight into action. The creamy mixture was heaped in silver dishes, half hidden under an overlying tracery of parsley. I was like a sprinter anticipating the starting pistol and, when guests were eventually seated, I eagerly reached out for the nearest dish.

Dainty portions of brown bread and Melba toast were handed round. I helped myself to a liberal portion of horseradish sauce. My dinner companion was very loquacious, relating his holiday experiences in India and was content with a few muttered interjections from me. I did not want to make conversation. I only wanted to savour to the full every succulent mouthful. As I scooped up the last morsel, topping it with a remaining blob of sauce and some parsley decoration, I became aware that side plates were being collected.

To my horror, I saw that there were only four dishes, including mine. I did a rapid mathematical calculation. Eight guests, four dishes.

Too late, I realised my horrendous mistake. It was obvious to me then that guests helped themselves to a portion of pâté from the dishes. I had consumed a whole dish. Should I apologise or should I act as though nothing happened? I adopted the latter course as, handing over my empty dish, I simply remarked that the pâté was absolutely superb. Fixing me with steely eyes, her voice loaded with asperity, my hostess replied, '*You* certainly enjoyed it, dear!' The word 'you' being heavily enunciated.

I have never felt quite the same about mackerel pâté since that unfortunate faux pas.

A most embarrassing and disappointing incident took place when I was serving with the ATS in Brussels during the latter part of the war.

Now, I know it is normal when greeting an acquaintance to do so in the upright position, but I managed the opposite one day when going shopping with a friend in the city. We were riding on a tram, a most hazardous occupation on the continent, when I recognised a familiar figure from my hometown, walking with a companion. He was the brother of a school friend, but we had not met for several years. He was nicknamed 'Jumbo' because of his great height and girth.

'I've got a date, see you later,' I shouted to my pal.

The tram had obligingly slowed down and, desperate that I might lose sight of him if I went on to the next stop, I jumped off. Now, trams on the continent have nasty little minds, being as capricious as a woman. As I leapt, the vehicle suddenly accelerated, flinging me out onto the pavement, where I lay spread-eagled in the path of my advancing prey. He gazed down at me from a great height. I must have looked a sight.

It had been raining and my skirt, revealing more khaki issue than decorum demanded, was mud spattered. I had lost a shoe. My stockings were laddered, my tie askew and my cap had fallen over one eye. Jumbo did not recognise me as, hauling me to my feet, he bellowed, 'You stupid girl, you might have been killed. Let that be a lesson to you!' And, having ascertained that I was all in one piece, he marched off into the crowd.

My collection includes an incident which, with hindsight, is very laughable, but I did not find it so at the time.

In the early war days, I worked as a volunteer nurse. My first morning on the ward was a disaster. I was not, of course, familiar with the appliance for emptying bedpans and felt very apprehensive when called upon to carry out this duty. I made my way to the sluice and, inserting the pan into the machine, closed the front loading door, pulling down the handle. But, horror of horrors, I had not shut the door properly. For it clanged open, shooting scalding water all over my person.

Now, in those days, nurses' uniforms were not sensible like those of today. Then, everything was starched – caps, cuffs, collars, belts, dresses and aprons. Consequently, my uniform was reduced to a limp, soggy mess.

Dissolving into tears, I ran, dripping water, down the long ward, to the accompaniment of whistles, yells and lewd innuendos from the patients who, being military personnel, never lost an opportunity to rag their nurses.

I would like to say I have discontinued my strange collecting habit, but fear this is not so. Why, only the other day…

Growing Pains

When Noel had left the village to study at an agricultural college in the north, he and Becky had decided to become engaged when she was twenty-one. They had known each other for several years and both their families were delighted. Now Becky herself was leaving for a three-year course at a university in the west of England. Noel had been home for a short summer holiday and they would not meet again until Christmas.

For the first few days, Becky found life at university very strange and bewildering, but after a couple of weeks she gradually found her feet.

It was when she was returning home from the library one afternoon that she met Gary. Her bicycle had struck a stone and she had fallen heavily into the gutter. He had picked her up and insisted on wheeling her bike back to college. Her heart had turned a sort of somersault when she had seen him bending over her. His blue eyes twinkled merrily and his tanned complexion, strong features and blond, curly hair reminded her of an Adonis.

'See you around,' he had said when he left her.

A few days later, she saw him in the cafeteria and they shared a table. He told her he was studying for a Ph.D. He hoped she was settling down and had made some friends. Perhaps he would see her at the disco being held at a nearby college on the following Saturday, he suggested. Becky was thrilled. She could not understand why he had singled her out.

However, when he took the floor with her at the disco, she knew she was falling in love with him, though she felt very guilty thinking of Noel so far away. But she pushed the feeling aside and gave herself up to the joy of the moment.

Several days went by before she saw him again. She had joined the walkers' club and was delighted when she found he was also one of a group assembled that Saturday for a day's trek into the countryside. She was blissfully happy when he chose to walk with her and remained by her side all day.

Thinking about him later, she wondered why he never made a definite date with her and why, although solicitous and charming, he had never kissed her. Her face flamed when she thought of those few seconds he had held her when lifting her down from a high gate on the walk; she fancied he had held her for longer than was necessary. Surely he had felt the pounding of her heart. Her whole body had tensed with excitement.

It was when she was in the games room that she heard some of the students talking about him.

'Lucky old Julia,' one of them was saying, 'wish I was in her shoes.'

'Fancy hooking the gorgeous Gary,' another remarked.

'Who's Julia?' asked Becky, alarmed.

'Oh, she graduated last year,' someone told her. 'Now she's working as a journalist in London. They met while studying here and plan to marry as soon as Gary gets his Ph.D.'

'You do mean Gary Summers?' Becky asked, her stomach muscles tightening with apprehension.

'The one and only,' they chorused.

'Hey,' one of them said, 'we've seen you and him together. He hasn't been leading you on, has he?'

'Of course not,' Becky replied hastily. 'We're only friends.'

Later, in her room, she cried into her pillow. Why had he not mentioned he already had a serious commitment? Now she understood why he had not treated her as a normal boyfriend would have done. She felt her world had fallen apart.

She took care to avoid him over the next few days and when Philip, a notorious charmer, asked her for a date, she agreed right away. He was great fun and soon began driving her out to small country pubs for evening meals, in his bright yellow sports car.

One day he asked her to go away with him for a weekend. They would stay at his aunt's apartment on the coast. 'You'll like her,' he said. 'She's marvellous company and has a great sense of humour.'

In addition to her feelings of guilt where Noel was concerned, Becky experienced a small pinprick of doubt. After all, she did not really know Philip all that well and there was talk about him, but if his aunt was there, she reassured herself, surely there was no harm.

However, the day before she was to leave for the weekend, she bumped into Gary. She tried to ignore him, but he quickly caught hold of her arm, saying, 'I haven't seen you lately, Becky. Please don't think I'm interfering, but a word of warning. I hear you're seeing a lot of Philip Wise. Just be careful, he's not your type.'

'Don't worry, I can look after myself,' she had retorted angrily as, tossing her head, she had walked rapidly away.

The following day, Philip picked her up in his sports car and, after a leisurely lunch at a quaint inn on the journey down, they reached their destination in the early afternoon.

Becky was rather taken aback that the aunt was not there to greet them, but felt sure she would be in later. The apartment was sumptuous, expensively curtained and carpeted, the furniture superb.

Philip showed her into his aunt's bedroom to freshen up. Having changed into a soft, pink woollen dress, she went into the lounge. The wine which Philip had plied her with at lunch had made her face glow and she felt a little unsteady. Romantic, dreamy music was coming from a music centre.

Then she heard Philip's voice.

'Come on, old girl,' he called, 'I'm in here.'

She moved across to the hall and, on opening a door, found herself in a double bedroom. Mirrors lined the walls. The furnishings, in a soft shade of apricot, were plush. Philip, naked, was lying on the satin quilt.

It took her a few seconds to sum up the situation.

'Where is your aunt?' she demanded, trembling with fury. 'I wouldn't have agreed to come away with you if I'd known she would not be here.'

'Don't be so silly, the dear aunt is safe in Florida and not expected back for at least a month. I say, you haven't been leading me on, have you?' Philip sounded very aggrieved.

'I'm going back to college,' she shouted, angrily slamming the door.

'Little bitch!' she heard him shout.

At the railway station, she was just in time to catch the 3.30 train.

Back at the college, she was confronted by Rogers, the porter. He had been working in the lodge for a great many years and there was not much he did not know about the students. Most of them confided in him while he, in turn, treated them rather like a benign father. He had seen Philip pick Becky up that morning and had put two and two together. Thus, being a good judge of character, he was not at all surprised to see her returning early.

'Thought you'd gone off for the weekend, miss,' he remarked.

'I changed my mind, Rogers,' she answered.

'Well, miss, that's lucky for someone, because there's a young gentleman by the name of Noel in the visitor's lounge, waiting to see you. He asked how long you'd be so I told him to wait a little while. I was pretty sure you'd show up shortly. But, miss, leave that overnight bag with me, eh! Better not let the young gentleman see it.'

'Oh Rogers, you are a dear,' Becky exclaimed.

She ran along the corridor and in her heart a little bird began to sing.

He was standing with his back to her, reading some notices and did not hear her open the door. She called his name, then flew into his arms.

'I read between the lines in your recent letters,' he explained eventually. 'And I was very worried because you sounded so depressed. I decided you needed cheering up, so here I am.'

'Oh Noel,' she sighed. 'I've been such a fool, but I'm fine now; and Noel, I love you so much, darling.'

Christmas Reminiscences

The word Christmas fills us with us with all sorts of thoughts and images and the more we think about it, the more actively our subconscious mind reacts, spilling out stored memories of festive seasons stretching far back to the shadowy past years of our youth.

For me, the highlight of Christmas is not Christmas Day but Christmas Eve. Ever since I was a child, this particular day has always held a certain fascination for me.

I try to finish my tasks early so that I am free to attend to my baking session after lunch. As I sift, crumble and roll, I listen to the Service of Nine Carols from King's College Chapel, Cambridge. The old familiar hymns ringing out their Christmas message recall incidents and scenes of the faraway past as vividly as though they had only recently occurred. The present becomes a blur as, like surf receding on the seashore, my thoughts flow back to the years of my youth. My surroundings become vague and indistinct. Only the past is real.

I see a small room lit by a large brass oil lamp and a spluttering, sizzling log fire. I am three years old. From tinselled branches of a small Christmas tree, pink and white sugar mice dizzily dangle by thin, white tails.

'This one is yours and this one is yours,' says Mother as, cutting down two mice, she hands one each to my twin brother and me.

'Look,' exclaims my brother, excitedly, putting his mouse right under Father's nose.

Father thinks he says, 'Bite', and promptly obeys by decapitating the proffered mouse with his teeth. Pandemonium breaks loose. Father shrieks with laughter, Mother scolds, the baby screams and my brother yells so loudly that all the tinsel on the little tree quivers and shivers in sympathy at the outrage.

The scene vanishes and is replaced by the sight of stockings hanging from black bed knobs, secured by large loops made from wide white tape. The stockings are unique. The legs, made of wool, are very long, very thick and black as pitch. The feet are silky soft and white as snow. Numerous nocturnal raids on them reveal nothing but, with the approach of dawn, their limpness mysteriously disappears. Now they bulge and are elongated, the feet all but reaching the floor.

When poked and prodded, all kinds of rustling sounds are produced. Plumbing their cavernous depths with eager fingers proves a feat of endurance not be to be abandoned until the last nut has been triumphantly retrieved.

My mother speaks. 'Tom,' she is saying, 'please get the tree decorations down from the loft.'

Excitement mounts as Dad appears with the precious big brown box. From musty smelling, yellowing tissue paper tumble half-forgotten treasures. It is like meeting dear old friends. Here is the cardboard-winged, silver-encrusted angel, each year losing more of her encrustations. The pink peacock, still proud though tailless. Little lanterns hung by small chains and shiny red, blue and gold miniature bugles.

The climax comes when the lid from a stout cardboard box is removed. The box is labelled 'Boots, black leather, size 9, price 5/6½p' and belies its contents, for inside reposes a flaxen-haired fairy doll, resplendent in a white frilly, sequined gown. On her head she wears a silver tiara and in her hand she carries a silver wand. She is very beautiful though it is sad to see her freshness slowly fading from the effects of her yearly incarceration.

Oh look, there is Mum again draped in a large, flower-sprigged apron. She is flushed and dishevelled from her ministrations of mixing, shredding and beating. 'Come and stir the Christmas pudding and make a wish, children,' she calls.

'Tell us your wish, come on,' my sisters beg.

'Shan't tell you, so there,' I say. 'It's a secret.'

'Bet you made two wishes, bet you did,' they say. 'Mum, she cheated.'

The clamour of ringing bells fills my ears. They are calling us to the church, their strident notes cutting the crisp night air. I feel very grown-up. This is my first Christmas Eve service. It is nearly midnight and very dark. Inside the church it is warm and full of light. Our eyes blink in the brilliance.

Soft music swells from the organ; the shining candles flicker. Starched surplices rustle as small boys take their places in the choir stalls, their faces cleanly scrubbed, their cheeks shining like polished holly berries. How quiet it is. Listen! They are singing a lullaby.

Down the corridors of time I see a shepherd approaching. Why, it is Dad. He is performing in the Nativity play and entering into the spirit of the occasion with remarkable enthusiasm considering the difficulty Mum had in persuading him to participate. He comes nearer and I see he is wrapped in a grey- and red-striped blanket. I remember Mum bought it in a Gamages sale. Under his left arm, he carries my sister's dilapidated woolly lamb; in his right hand, he carries a crook.

Oh dear! A large safety pin has become unfastened and part of the blanket has fallen away, revealing two elegant, snow-white long john-clad legs. My mother is mortified, but Dad, oblivious of the predicament, is singing lustily: 'It came upon the midnight clear, that glorious song of old'.

A door slams and the past fades. Only my mind has been far, far away. My hands have been busy performing their tasks and I nibble a hot mince pie as I fill the kettle for tea.

Death on the High Street

The last thing she remembered was the harsh screech of brakes, followed by a sensation of falling headlong into a tunnel, down, down, down.

She tried to think clearly. Where was she? What was happening to her?

Ah, that was it. She had been on her way up the high street to post some letters before a visit to the dentist. She had seen the postman across the road, emptying the post box and had rushed over. The November afternoon had been fading fast. A slight drizzle fell, making the road surface shiny and slippery.

She could not have posted the letters, neither had she reached the dentist.

A terrible thought struck her. The screeching brakes meant an accident. She was the victim, knocked down by a passing car. Why then was there no pain?

Then she heard a voice. 'She's gone,' it said.

Panic seized her. She must be dead, but if she was dead, how could she hear, how think?

She opened her mouth to speak, to tell 'them' she was still alive, but no sound came. She tried to move, but her body felt heavy, like lead, refusing to obey her instructions.

She had read a story once about a driver involved in an accident and certified dead. But he was not dead, though how was he to let them know? Eventually, he had managed to move a little finger and kept twitching it, but no one had noticed and he had been taken to the mortuary where he had been covered with a sheet. Later, when his parents arrived to identify him and he had seen their terrible sadness, his eyes had miraculously filled with tears. Only then had it been realised that he was still alive.

She must cry. But tears did not come easily. Quick, think of something sad. Yes, the lovely new white dress embroidered with pink flowers hanging in her wardrobe ready for the forthcoming Christmas dance. She would never get to wear it now. A great sadness swept over her.

It was not fair. She was only seventeen, too young to die. Anger replaced sadness and no tears fell.

Perhaps she ought to pray. 'Our Father which art in Heaven,' she began, but when she came to 'Give us this day our daily bread,' she had an idea. Think about food. Maybe she would dribble and it would be noticed.

Oh, those delicious slices of roast beef – Dad carving her off a second helping, adding the last piece of Yorkshire pudding; the mouth-watering juices from the joint poured on top. But no action was taken so she obviously had not dribbled.

'Forgive us our trespasses,' she continued, then paused. Had she been very wicked? Surely not, well, not too wicked.

There had been the affair of the worm. A big, fat juicy one she had dug up specially and impaled with a large safety pin, securing it into the autograph book belonging to Maggie Stevens, who was terrified of worms. What a dreadful thing to do. She felt so ashamed.

'Lead us not into temptation.' Would she stand accused of that particular crime? She was afraid so. How often, when appearing to listen carefully to the Sunday sermon, had she spent the time fantasising over one of the choirboys, so dark, so handsome? How very irreverent.

Why was it so quiet? She must be in limbo. Perhaps they of the realms above were even now going through her records and she was being assessed. If only she could write a letter.

Dear Sir, or To Whom It May Concern

I feel sure a mistake has been made. I should not be dead. My death is very untimely. Please look into this matter immediately and amend your records accordingly.

How should she sign it? 'Yours humbly'? 'Yours in haste'? She could not make up her mind.

Then suddenly she was rushing back up the tunnel. A light shone at the entrance.

'Come along, young lady,' someone said. 'It's all over.'

Feeling dopey, she slowly opened her eyes and recognised the dentist.

A great surge of relief flooded through her like a huge tidal wave. She was alive! She was alive!

Giggling foolishly, she heard herself stammer weakly, 'I, I've had a t'terrible maresnight.'

Yesterday

A strange thing happened today when I gazed into my mirror. The glass appeared to ripple. My image became indistinct and, when it cleared, I saw the reflection of myself as a young girl of seventeen.

Memories flooded in back to over fifty years ago to the time before our peaceful country erupted in the flames of war and the killings and the heartbreak began.

At that time, I worked in the counting house of a large department store. In those days, it was not called an office. Wages were low; hours long. I began my apprenticeship, as it was called then, at 5/- a week. The store closed for one half day a week and holidays consisted of one week a year. The working day for juniors began at 8.30.

On Mondays and Tuesdays the store closed at 6 p.m., on Wednesdays at 1 p.m., and on Thursdays and Fridays at 7 p.m. On Saturdays it was 8 p.m. However, in spite of the low pay and long hours, which must by today's standards seem harsh, I was very happy and carefree.

Whenever I had to go into the store, it was necessary to negotiate steep, rickety, wooden stairs, but what a feast of delights met my eye in all departments. To me it was like going into Aladdin's cave. There were so many lovely things. Gorgeous hats ranging in price from 4/6d to several guineas each. Beautiful materials – pretty flowered cottons from 1/11¾d a yard, expensive, exotic silks and brocades, smart afternoon and evening dresses, as well as sheer silk lingerie. I would gaze longingly at all these luxuries, knowing that I could never afford to buy.

Behind the scenes, tucked away out of sight, two girls sat in a tiny room, making hats to order and, nearby in another room, others sat at long tables, sewing garments for the well-to-do, their heads assiduously bent over their work. The head of department sat erect as a ramrod, watching every move. The room always seemed to be full of steam caused by one of the workers ironing over a damp cloth.

I was terrified of all the buyers. They seemed such superior beings.

Miss Woodward, an elderly spinster – we nicknamed her 'Tilly' behind her back – ruled over us girls in the counting house with a rod of iron, lashing out with her tongue if any of us dared turn up a minute late. A stout lady, well upholstered and with a mass of iron-grey hair, she exuded discipline, nothing escaping her eagle eye.

What a thrill it was to save up for something new. I remember, after putting 1/- away for many weeks, being able to afford to purchase a very fashionable camel-colour swagger coat, priced at 21/-; I felt like a queen when I wore it. No garment bought since has ever given me so much pleasure.

At seventeen, I experienced my first romance. He was Welsh, several years my senior and worked on the local newspaper. My parents and he had many heated arguments over politics – he read The Daily Worker, they took The Daily Mail, or The Telegraph when they could afford it. Every Saturday he met me from work and took me to the pictures, or the flicks as it was then called. He always presented me with a large box of chocolates and I felt very grown-up and sophisticated.

However, as time passed and in order to retain my virginity, I had to give up the Welshman, the chocolates and the Saturday cinema treat. I was not unduly upset, as I had, by now, set my sights on a young apprentice who worked in the furnishing department.

Later that year, I attended my first big dance held at the main hotel in the town. Mother took me up to London to a Guinea Gown shop, where I chose a dream of a dress in white satin. The sleeves were puffed, the neckline demure and tiny sprays of forget-me-nots peeped out of ruche ribbon on the sleeves and skirt. My twin brother was to chaperone me and wore a new suit for the occasion, a bit on the large side, but Mother said he would grow into it as time went on. The trouble was that he took his job of chaperoning much too seriously for my liking.

'Don't flirt or make dates with anyone and don't forget you're coming home with me,' he warned. In spite of this, I had a simply wonderful time, even managing a couple of furtive kisses from partners, behind potted palms.

Christmas in the store was full of bustle and excitement, the shop lavishly garlanded and decorated for the festive season. In spite of our low wages, we in the counting house managed to buy each other a small gift and Tilly would allow us to leave our work while we excitedly undid our gifts, which were wrapped in tissue or brown paper. No coloured ribbon, glittering tape or pretty Christmas paper. We certainly could not have afforded such things.

What a feast Mother prepared for our Christmas dinner, the only time of the year when we enjoyed a plump, stuffed chicken. How delicious the pudding, all the more tasty because we had all had a hand in the making of it. I loathed stoning the large raisins – such a messy job – but much enjoyed the task of cutting up the large pieces of sugared candied peel, popping lumps of the delicious sugar in my mouth when I thought no one was looking.

The store only closed on Christmas Day and Boxing Day, then it was back at work for stocktaking, which kept us very busy. At the start of the New Year, we were called in turn to one of the directors for a pep talk, when he would inform us about our rises, usually 2/6d a week. We thought we were rich indeed.

That was the year of 1937 when I bought my first bicycle on the hire purchase (HP), much against my father's wishes, as he did not agree with having things on HP. The price, if I remember rightly, was £7.50 (in today's money) and the bike gave me so much pleasure and was worth every penny. What glorious rides my friends and I enjoyed, cycling along the Kentish lanes, so much safer in those days when there was so little traffic on the roads.

This was a lovely, happy era for me when the world, seen through the eyes of a seventeen year old, was tinged with a rosy glow and the future beckoned full of adventure with no premonition of the heartbreak and upheaval a war, only two years distant, would bring.

But now the glass ripples again. I am transported back to the here and now. Gone are the bright eyes, the youthful, expectant expression, the dark, shining hair and I write the following with an aching heart, for:

I see reflected in my glass
A mask, a mask of age,
A stranger looking out at me
With wrinkled skin and fading eyes,
Hair silver-grey.
And I cried aloud for all
My yesterdays,
But the face in the mirror mocked my tears
And as I stared into its depths,
I knew it told no lies.

A First Memory

I've been with her many, many years. You see, I'm her brain, stuffed full of memories, all neatly catalogued, filed, you might say, in chronological order. Sometimes, we get rather impatient when we can't find the right file. You see, she's getting on a bit now so I'm apt to feel a bit top-heavy, but we can go back a very long way. Back in time down long corridors still echoing with sounds of days long gone, evoking sad and happy occasions.

Let's go back to the time when she was only knee-high to a daffodil, to a sunny day in March, when, dressed in a crisp, white pinafore, she toddled down the garden path with Alice, several years her senior. The wind has caught Alice's flaxen hair and it blows it round her pretty face like a halo. She swings a basket back and forth as she skips along.

'Will you show me the blackbird nest, Alice?' the little one asks.

'Later,' Alice answers. 'First we must go to the farm.'

We remember that day particularly, because it seemed a special sort of golden day at first. The bright sunshine, the celandines glowing in the grass like myriads of tiny stars and huge mustard colour kingcups on the margin of the stream, whose surface scintillated and flashed.

At the farm, the girls drink golden, creamy milk, fresh from buttercup-field cows, and eat yellow, buttery scones, still hot from the big cooking range.

Now the farmer's wife is taking them to the dairy, where large round straw-coloured cheeses are maturing on burnished wooden racks. She cuts a large hunk from one of them, which Alice pops into her basket. From the henhouse, they collect honey-brown eggs.

'When can we see the nest?' the little one, who is only knee-high to a daffodil, asks impatiently, prompted by me, her brain.

'It's just up the lane, come on.' Waving goodbye to the farmer's wife, the two children set off home.

The nest is high up in the hedge, which is studded all over with lush, green tips.

'I'll have to pick you up so that you can see it.' And Alice takes the little one in her arms, lifting her up so that her face is level with the nest.

'Oh, it's got eggs in it. Can I have one?' And, before Alice can reply, a chubby hand takes out a speckled egg. Alas, she holds it too tightly and, at that moment, the golden day erupts in a stream of bright-orange yolk, which dribbles all down the crisp, white pinny.

'You wicked girl,' Alice shrieks. 'You've killed a bird and just look at your pinny!'

The little one sobs. She's engulfed in waves of remorse and will never forget the day her clumsy fingers destroyed a precious egg, which deprived a blackbird of life. The day, when, although only knee-high to a daffodil, she first met guilt face to face.

Birdsgrove

Nurse says it's a lovely day, warm for the time of year; tells us there are snowdrops in the flowerbeds. Wish I could see them, but for all of us in here, age clamps us to our chairs. Most we manage is totter to meals and bed, though some do need a helping hand, or push walking frames.

How long have I been in here? Seems like forever. Is there another world out there? Trouble is you get institutionalised after a while. What is outside these walls ceases to bother you. Here we live from one meal to the next.

I'm luckier than some. Still able to read. Only big print books, mind you. Didn't like them, at first. They're kids' books, I said. Wasn't having them, but came to it in the end. Got a real nice one this week – HE Bates. Ever so naughty. Going to get them to renew it so I can have another read.

Some of us get visitors, but others have outlived their families and friends. Sad.

Violet sits next to me. She's ninety. Wish she wouldn't repeat herself. Keeps on saying, 'I was with my lady for thirty-five years,' and 'Do you know Eastbourne?' It gets so boring. Sometimes I get cross and tell her to keep quiet. Once I got really mad and said, 'Why don't you belt up?'

But it didn't make any difference. Never seems to dress herself properly. Just look at her. One knicker leg showing and half the buttons of her dress undone. Can't think how she managed 'my lady' all those years. Ties string round her handbag – says that'll stop people getting their thieving hands on it. Silly old woman.

Martha sits the other side of me. She's ninety-three. Nice little party. Knits squares for blankets all day, not to mention dishcloths. Deaf as a post. Always gives me the wrong answer when I ask her anything so I don't bother now, but just let her prattle on.

Now, Lily over there: very good sense of humour, I'll say that for her, but so rude. Always belching. Never apologises, just laughs at herself. Downright disgusting, I call it.

Here comes Nurse. I know just what she's about to say. 'Does anyone need the toilet? Now, we don't want any little accidents, do we!' Treat you like you're in the nursery, they do. I tell her straight that if I want the toilet, I don't need reminding, thank you.

Get too much time to think, in here. Trouble is, although our bodies age, memories of days gone by get more vivid, sort of tantalisingly linger. One feeds on the memory. Remembering brings pain, thinking of all the lovely people. What was that poem I learnt all those years ago at school? Let me think now. Ah yes, I know. I believe it was called 'Twilight' by John Masefield and went like this:

> I think of the friends who are dead,
> Who were dear long ago in the past,
> Beautiful friends who are dead
> Though I know that death cannot last,
> Friends with the beautiful eyes

That the dust hath defiled,
Beautiful friends who were gentle
When I was child.

Fancy me being able to call it to mind after all these years.

'No, Nurse, I'm not crying. Just got an itchy eye. No, it's quite all right, I'm fine.'

They're coming round with the pills. Often wonder what's the point of keeping us all going. Gave us flu jabs last week. Now we've all gone down with a cold. Still, I suppose they've got to keep us going. Look bad if we popped our clogs for want of pills and things. Give the papers a field day. A real scandal, there'd be.

Got a bottle of brandy in my bag. Often have a sly swig. My son slips it in when he visits. Well, they say a little of what you fancy does you good. Reckon it's pickling my old bones, that's for sure.

There's a rumour, only a rumour, mind you, that we're having some gentlemen inmates soon. On the strength of that, I've booked a perm with the visiting hairdresser. Be interesting getting male company after all this time. Quite exciting.

There goes the bell for lunch. Pork today, they say. Hope there's apple sauce. Wish they wouldn't make us wear those awful bibs. I ask you, it's humiliating. Treat us like babies, they do.

Mary sits next to me at table. Quite good manners, not like some I could name. Pity she's such a noisy eater. Teeth a bad fit. It's clack, clack all through the meal.

Still, mustn't grumble. It's warm and comfy here. Grub's not bad and they're kind. After all, what can one expect at our time of life? Tell me, I'll be getting the telegram soon. Who'd have thought I'd live to such a great age? Oh well, I know I'm going to enjoy that pork. Right now, life's not bad, not bad at all.

Heatwave

Saffron sun blazing, boiling and bubbling,
Airwaves pulsating, droning and humming,
Doves moaning and cooing,
Larks soaring and singing,
Marigolds shouting.
Motorways choking, snarling coast-wards,
Horns honking,
Brakes screeching,
Sirens wailing,
Someone screaming,
Sweat dripping,
Timbers creaking, contracting.
Heat spewing, spiralling upwards,
Motor mowers rotating,
Ice cream vans vociferating.
Kids plashing and paddling in mussled and
    winkled pools.
Hot breezes flapping and furling sandcastle
    flags,
Gulls squawking and squabbling over
    yesterday's crumbs.
Ticket machines clicking,
Deckchairs scraping,
Holidaymakers guzzling, scrunching and
    munching.
Hurdy-gurdies jangling,
Brass bands blaring.

Lovers tittering, tumbling in tall grass.
Leather thwacking on willow,
Teacups tinkling,
Thunder rumbling,
Lightning spluttering,
Raindrops spattering
And a nightingale singing in a Surrey wood.

Come Death, but Not Too Soon

*(Dedicated to a lady who died in her
one-hundredth year)*

Alone... Alone... I sit here alone,
For all of my own have now gone.
Why do I linger? I'm old and so tired
And all of my own have now died.

Come Death, haste and cover me up with your
  mantle,
Close my eyes, stop my feeble heart beating.
My husband, my children, my friends who
  were gentle,
Have left me alone now and silently grieving.

I smoulder with longing to slough off life's
  burden,
To lay down beside them,
The ones I once lived for
And now wish to die for.

I shed tears of sorrow,
Oh, hasten tomorrow,
Come, Death, freeze my old veins,
My joints quickly stiffen.

I long to be with them,
The loved ones I lived for –
I still hear their voices,
Their shadowy faces flit ghostly before me.

But listen!
    A blackbird
        Is singing
            A love song,

And crocuses
    Are golden
        Outside in my garden.

Stay, Death, come no nearer;
I'll rest here a while, for
The sunshine is warmer
Than your icy finger.

Pray, go now, don't linger.
Perhaps next November
I'll summon you hither.
Right now, I've decided to live a bit longer.

WI Market

Every Friday in the morning
In the little town of Verwood
Flourishes a WI market.
Very busy is that market,
Many people go to buy there.
Buyers queue up very early
For to purchase local produce –
Carrots, leeks, potatoes, spinach,
Marrows, turnips, parsnips, lettuce
And in season all the soft fruits.

Members bake delicious goodies,
Fruit cakes, jam tarts, pastries, sponges,
Cakes of almond, iced cakes, quiches,
Apple pies, meringues and jams.

Other goods are on display there.
Teapot cosies, woolly jumpers,
Soft toys, bed socks, aprons floral,
Eggs so fresh, both small and large size.
Plentiful are all the plants there –
Heathers, cactus, shrubs so various,
Flower arrangements in profusion.

All the buyers must be fearless
To withstand the crush of bodies,
Jabs with elbows, shopping baskets.

But you must be very careful
When first you select your purchase
And are ready with your money.
Hold on tight or you may find that
Someone else will whip your produce!

When you have your shopping finished
And your cash is running low,
You might find an empty table
For a little light refreshment,
Biscuits, soft drinks, tea or coffee.
Necessary is that respite
After all the rush and turmoil,
Ere you wend your journey homeward,
Ere again you take the high road,
Loaded up with all the goodies
Made and grown by clever members
Of that body so fraternal,
Of that body meritorious,
WI market, Verwood, Dorset.

Stubs

Spent stubs in the park
Hundreds of stubs
Littering the grass
Remnants of weeds
Weeds of disease
Incongruous
Ominous
Bodily poison
Nicotine toxin
Fouling
Begriming
Oxygen stealing
Life force destroying.

When will they learn
Smoking to spurn?
When comprehend
The medical warning
The frightening warning
That cigarette
Smoking
Kills?

The Miracle of Life

(Call it Evolution or Creation)

Is
The scented petal of a rose,
A snowdrop peeping through the snow,
The tinkle of a bluebell's ring,
Poppies in a field of corn.
A pretty, timid, dappled fawn,
A sunflower, stately, golden crowned,
Chestnut trees in summer gown,
A rabbit nibbling fresh green grass,
A killer whale in oceans deep
And birds that sweetly pipe and cheep.

But the most marvellous miracle of all
Is the babe born of man,
A human creation,
Able to build, invent and compose
For better or worse and shape our world.

Life's miracles are everywhere.
Do we take them for granted?
Do we ever spare
A thought for the wonderful
Gifts around us
And respectfully nurture
The magic we share?

But, alas, in our world
There are many who suffer
Abuse and neglect and terrible wars
And never find pleasure
In life's infinite treasures.

It's not fair, it's unjust
And one ponders and wonders
What life's all about.
And asks, *Why? Why? Why? Why?*

The Surgery

'Hello, Mrs Gunn,
Your appointment's at ten.
The doctor's not here,
I fear he slept in.'

So I sit on a bench
By a young buxom wench
And smile at her child
Who pokes out his tongue.
'Well! Well!' I declare,
'There are no manners there.'
Then I pick up a mag
Two years out of date.
Doctor really is late.

The time seems to lag
And oh, what a din!
Phones constantly ring.
I'll just listen in –
'Surgery here, surgery here.
I'm so sorry, dear.
You've had a bad fall.
You fell off a table.
Now, now, please don't worry.
Doctor will call
As soon as he's able.'
Ring-ring-ring-ring,

My head's in a spin.
'What's that – an infection?
No! You want an injection.
Yes, come to the clinic
To collect a prescription.'
'Surgery here, surgery here.
You've got diarrhoea.
Oh dear, it's your ear.
You must make an appointment.
It sounds very urgent.'
'Mrs Gunn, Mrs Gunn,
The doctor has come.'

So I rush down a corridor,
Which door – is it this door?
Not that one or that one.
Doctor! Oh Doctor!
Oh where is my doctor?
They've altered the clinic
Since I was last in it.
I'll try down this way.
My God, what a maze!
Ah! Here is the right door.

'So…sorry…Doctor…
I thought…I…had…lost yer…
I'm quite…out of…breath…'
'Now you know, Mrs Gunn,
There was no need to run.
It just isn't done at your age –
Now come over here
And sit on this chair.

Please bare your arm,
I've no doubt you've done harm.
Yes, just as I thought,
You're quite overwrought.
Come and see me again
And, my dear Mrs Gunn,
Remember: '*Don't* run…'

'Oh! Mrs Gunn, Mrs Gunn.
I've a terrible pain.
Oh! My dear Mrs Gunn,
Please hurry, run, run.
Fetch a doctor, quick, quick.
I feel very sick.
Mrs Gunn! Mrs Gunn!
Hurry, hurry – *Run, run*.'

The Magic of May: A Sonnet

The air was full of scents of summer flowers
And cuckoos called from far across the weald
And mauve wisteria made a secret bower
And buttercups glowed golden in the field,
When first I looked into your eyes so blue
And saw that roguish smile light up your face,
Then happiness suffused my body through.
I never, ever will forget that place
Where all the world was filled with saffron sun,
The day our years fell off like withered leaves.
Oh, how we laughed and loved and had such
    fun.
We cheated time, we were like naughty thieves
    –
That day in May will always be for me
A bittersweet and lovely memory.

Sales Talk

No one will ever force me into purchasing anything against my will, I have often remarked. That is, until the day I decided a really good moisturising cream was urgently needed for my complexion, in order, hopefully, to assuage time's ravages.

To this end, I took a trip to a high-class store. At the cosmetic counter displaying the particular brand I required, an exquisite vision confronted me, immaculately made up.

'Oh,' she cooed in honeyed tone in answer to my request. 'Madam has very good skin. I recommend this excellent cream.'

Now, I just love compliments and began purring inwardly.

'And, Madam,' she continued, 'this week we are offering a lovely free handbag if you also buy this special flacon of mousse make-up, which is applied over the cream. Madam's face will glow!'

The price was far, far more than I had expected or indeed had in my purse, but the trap was sprung and finally clicked shut, when she agreed to accept a cheque to cover the difference on production of my OAP railcard as identification, exclaiming incredulously that I looked far too young to be a pensioner. My purring increased in volume. I felt we were cocooned in an aura of mutual feline satisfaction.

Once outside the store, cold reality hit me. I had grossly overspent, including all the housekeeping money for the rest of the month. And the handbag, which had appeared sleek and sophisticated cunningly displayed against a background of plush, cream velvet, now lay limp and uninteresting in the bottom of the smart carrier bag provided by the store.

I then realised I had been a willing victim of sales talk and, to make matters worse, my husband says he sees no difference between the expensive, newly bought cosmetics and the cheaper products I have used for years.

Elmo

It is some years since Elmo was finally banished to my bedroom, never to show his face again downstairs. Time and time again, Dad threatened to get rid of him and it is only due to Mum's repeated intervention that he still survives.

At this point, I should explain that Elmo is my teddy bear. He is made of black fur which, over the years, and because of his numerous escapades, is now much the worse for wear, being exceedingly dilapidated and bedraggled. Neither are his pink felt eyes the originals – the latter were discarded long ago for reasons I shall go into later. One ear is badly chewed and if you turn him over onto his tummy, you will feel a ridge down the middle of his back, indicating some past adversity.

I cannot remember life without Elmo. He has been part of it ever since I was a year old, although, at the time Aunt Mary presented him to me, it seems, according to Mum, I was much more interested in the paper he was wrapped in.

However, Elmo and I gradually became inseparable. He shared my bed and has always been my confidant and comforter but, unfortunately, he had a very strong will and, over the years, caused a great deal of trouble to lots of people, not least my parents.

Today, those pink eyes gaze at me accusingly from his perch on the bookshelf, where he lolls between a dog-eared copy of *Treasure Island* and *Gulliver's Travels*. Soon I leave home for college and he must remain behind. After all the trials and tribulations we have endured together and all the scrapes he has been involved in, I do not think it advisable to pack him in my holdall. It would be asking for trouble. The decision to leave him behind has been a difficult one. We have been through a great deal together, Elmo and I. I am sad to leave him.

I suppose Elmo's trouble began one day when Mum and I went shopping in the nearby town. Transport to and from our village is infrequent and, just as we were about to board the bus for the homeward journey, I screamed very loudly because Elmo was no longer with us. Mum was not a bit pleased.

'Where did you leave him?' she sighed as we retraced our steps up the high street.

'Don't know,' I replied.

Eventually, Elmo was located, sitting in the middle of the meat pie section in Marks and Spencer. How he got there, I really have no idea but, being full of curiosity, he was always poking his nose into things which did not concern him. Of course, we were late home and Dad's tea was not ready when he came in from work, so he was not pleased either.

Fortunately, we live in a small village, where everyone knows everyone else, so when Elmo wandered off, as he so frequently did, to loiter in local shops or lose himself at bazaars and garden fetes, he always found his way home. This sometimes involved a telephone call, after which either Mum or Dad would have to collect him, but often finders went out of their way to return him. Once, the vicar brought him back propped up in his bicycle basket.

One summer holiday while we were walking on the pier, Elmo, being of a somewhat venturesome nature, dived over the rail into the turbulent waves below. Dad had to pay a grumpy old man to take him out in a small boat to effect a rescue. Quite a crowd had gathered to watch and a cheer went up when Elmo was fished out of the water, but Dad, not being a good sailor, spent the journey back to the beach with his head stuck over the side of the heaving craft. He was really mad.

Then, one day, a calamity occurred, which was to land Elmo into further trouble at a later date. It so happened that my horrid, spoilt cousin came to visit with her equally obnoxious mother. We were told to go into the garden and amuse ourselves but, as usual, we quarrelled and I went off on my own. When I returned, I found Elmo oozing stuffing all over the patio from a large stab wound in his back. There was an awful commotion. Mum called the cousin a nasty, vicious child, the upshot being that the aunt never set foot in our house again. As she was Dad's sister, Elmo got the blame and, having alienated her, he went down further in Dad's estimation.

I nearly lost my Elmo for good when Mum was roped in to help run a Mother's Union jumble sale. Everyone was terribly busy sorting things out and I got dreadfully bored. I left Elmo on a trestle table while I retired into a corner to amuse myself with a jigsaw puzzle Mum had found for me. After completing it, I went to retrieve Elmo, but the table, which had earlier been comparatively clear, was now piled high with all manner of articles. In vain, I searched and questioned, but helpers said I was a nuisance and told me to run away as they had enough to do dealing with the surging throng intent on finding as many bargains as they could lay their hands on. I was elbowed, pushed and shoved around, but then, suddenly, I spotted Elmo's head sticking out of Mrs Henshaw's shopping basket.

He was squashed between a dingy lampshade and a gaudy china jug with a chipped spout. Mrs Henshaw is the village busybody and I did not like her very much. Clutching at her coat sleeve, I yelled, 'That's my bear you've got in there. Give it to me, please.'

'Yours?' she hissed. 'Who says so? I've paid good money for that bear. You can't have it.'

My screams brought Mum rushing over from where she was endeavouring to serve several people, all clamouring for attention. She looked flustered and irritable as she tried to explain that the bear had not been for sale, but that I had left it on the table by mistake. But Mrs Henshaw was immovable and it was only when Mum offered her far more than she had paid for Elmo that she grudgingly condescended to hand him over. As we were not exactly rolling in money – one of Dad's favourite expressions – neither Elmo nor I were popular for a long time.

Another trauma took place when Mum noticed that one of Elmo's eyes was missing.

'That bear had two eyes last night,' she said to Dad, and a frantic search ensued but to no avail.

'The child must have swallowed it,' she wailed and I was whisked off to the doctor and then admitted to the local hospital and put to bed on the children's ward for observation.

The following day, I confided to a pretty nurse who had taken a liking to Elmo, in spite of the fact that he was now eyeless, Mum having taken the precaution of removing his remaining eye.

'I've just remembered where Elmo's eye is,' I told her. 'I buried it in Mum's flowerpot.'

After they rang my home and it was confirmed that the eye was indeed under several inches of soil, I was rapidly bundled out of the ward. When Dad came in from work, I heard him shouting at Mum in the kitchen that that bloody bear was nothing but trouble and he was going on the next bonfire. Elmo and I made ourselves very scarce for a while after that.

To this day, I will never understand how Elmo hitched a ride on the refuse truck. I had wedged him between the spokes of our front gate while I called next door for my pal. When I came back he had vanished.

'He's gone off with the refuse man,' I cried, remembering that Mum had put out the rubbish bag that morning.

She was busy making pastry, but rushed down the road in hot pursuit of the truck, still wielding the rolling pin. Sure enough, there was Elmo sitting up in the cab as jaunty as you please. There was a lot of arguing between Mum and the driver, who said he was entitled to his perks. Mum threatened to ring the council and report him for stealing, but after more angry words and Mum parting with a tip, he let me have Elmo back.

I think the cliff episode was one of the worst in Elmo's life. Dad let my pal come on holiday with us. While playing catch with the bear as we were walking along the cliff path, Elmo must have got bored, because he suddenly disappeared over the edge. The cliff sloped away fairly gradually, but he had chosen to explore further down, where there was quite a steep drop. Another man and Dad gingerly clambered down to retrieve him, but Dad cannot stand heights and looked terrible. The man lost a shoe, which we heard clatter down to the shingle far below. His wife kept shouting at him not to be such a damn silly fool and to get back up immediately.

Although I was really worried about Elmo, it was all very exciting. Then a young chap came along who said he had done a lot of climbing and, in no time at all, Elmo and I were reunited. Dad's trousers were torn and his shirt was filthy. On top of that, he had to give the man some money so that he could buy a new pair of shoes.

'I'll hang for that bloody bear one of these days,' Dad fumed.

Perhaps I should relate how Elmo's ear came to be so badly chewed and the tip bitten right off.

Now, there is a mean sort of dog living at the end of our road. You have only got to look at him to see he is out for trouble by the way his top lip is set in a permanent snarl. Whenever anyone walks past his house, he emits a bad-tempered growl, then barks incessantly, at the same time hurling his great body at the gate.

I decided to give him a fright, so, securing a length of string round Elmo, I crept up to the gate and lowered him over the top; I then crouched down, out of sight. The dog rushed out to investigate, but stopped dead in his tracks at the sight of the pink-eyed Elmo. However, the owner must have been watching from the house, because she came running out.

'You nasty, beastly bear!' she screeched. 'How dare you frighten my darling Poochie Woochie. I'll report you to the RSPCA, that I will.'

I thought it a good idea at this point to make a strategic withdrawal, but Elmo was enjoying himself and slipped out of his restraining string. The dog, emboldened by the presence of his owner, leapt on Elmo, embedding its great fangs in one of his ears and shook him to and fro so violently that I was afraid my darling would surely disintegrate. I finally got him back when the owner managed to wrench him from those murderous jaws and fling him over the wall into the gutter. We gave that place a wide berth after that.

Elmo's final incarceration came about because of an incident at London Airport when we returned from a holiday abroad.

Dad went through the green light, but a zealous customs official carried out a spot check and he had to admit to bringing in two bottles of spirits over the limit. No doubt all would have been well if Elmo had not attracted attention to himself by collapsing onto the floor. As the customs man bent to pick him up, I told him to be very careful, explaining that my bear had been stabbed in the back and Mum had had to sew him up. I noticed a queer look on the man's face as his fingers found the site of Mum's ministrations.

Things happened very quickly after that. Mum and I found ourselves seated in a corridor with a customs lady. Dad was taken away. Elmo was taken away too.

'I want Elmo!' I shrieked.

'Be quiet,' Mum whispered. She looked ever so upset and I got a bit worried.

When Dad finally appeared, his face was ever so red. He was clutching a large paper bag, which I learnt later contained Elmo, now in need of further surgery. Dad stormed out of the building and, as we trailed after him, we heard him muttering between clenched teeth that the bloody bear would be the death of him. 'Either it goes or I go,' I heard him say. 'And I never want to set eyes on him again.'

After that terrible episode, Mum made quite sure I kept Elmo in my bedroom, out of sight. If he ever came out, she swore she would not be responsible for his safety.

Now the time has come to say goodbye. We have been through a lot together, old pal, and despite all the trouble you have caused, you will always be my beloved friend.

Operation Bird Bath

The deserted London streets shone wetly in the glow of street lamps, which glimmered hazily in the murky November drizzle. The time was 7.30 p.m. Workers had departed, leaving shops and offices deserted, but from the half-lit interior of a high-class gents' outfitters, the figure of a man emerged in the window. Deftly, he undressed one of the models attired in a Burberry overcoat and tweed cap, placing it behind him on the shop floor. He then divested himself of his outer garments, replacing them with those he had taken from the model. However, when he came to put on the brogues the model had worn, he found, to his annoyance, that they were far too small, so, reluctantly, put his own black shoes back on.

Fred, alias The Squirrel, thought he cut quite a dash. Clean shaven, even featured and with a somewhat vacant expression, he was admirably cut out for the pose of a tailor's dummy. He, together with Mick, alias Small Boy, planned to assassinate the Prime Minister on her way to a banquet being held that very evening in the Guildhall. If their plan succeeded, it would be the last job they would pull. With the rake-off they would receive, they could retire abroad and live in luxury for the rest of their lives.

Fred switched on a radio concealed under his coat and spoke into it.

'Hello, Small Boy. Are you receiving me?'

'Receiving you, Squirrel. Am in position,' the answer came back.

'Good, Small Boy. I will inform you when Bird Bath passes, which should be in about twenty minutes from now. Understood?'

'OK, Squirrel,' replied Small Boy.

It had all been too easy, thought Fred. The months of planning were paying off. After much deliberation, he had chosen this particular vantage point where he could easily see oncoming traffic and had visited the shop several times to make purchases, always differently disguised. With his usual dexterity, he had got hold of the shop keys and, while in the fitting room, had made impressions of the keys. Not for nothing was he known in the criminal world as Fingers Fred.

Bird Bath had been his idea of a code name for the Prime Minister's car. The banquet was scheduled to commence at 8 p.m. Careful planning and timing, together with up-to-date information of the route the PM's car would take, had enabled him to anticipate, within a few seconds, the exact moment the car would pass the shop. He would call up Small Boy who, from his hidden vantage point on the flat roof further down the street, would aim down onto the car as it passed beneath him. Small Boy had a well thought out escape route planned, while Squirrel would re-dress the dummy and disappear through the rear of the shop to make a clean getaway through the back streets.

Only ten minutes to go, Fred said to himself, but then, to his consternation, he saw two policemen turn the corner and walk towards the shop where he was staked out. He stiffened, then froze, as one of them stopped and looked into the window. He broke out into a cold sweat and held his breath.

Now, PC Chalmers had an eye for expensive clothes, but on his pay could ill afford the prices of the garments on sale in this particular outfitters. Nevertheless, he had occasionally made the odd small purchase there. He was very interested in the Burberry worn by the model in the middle of the window.

'Come on,' his companion said. 'You know you can't afford these prices.'

But PC Chalmers had noticed something strange, for, not only was he a connoisseur of good clothes, he was also a keenly observant character, possessing an exceptionally analytical brain which his training had further sharpened. He knew quite well that a window dresser would never dress a model in that particular outfit, wearing those black shoes. It was all wrong. His mind began clicking with computer-like precision. As he turned away, he could swear the eyes of the dummy blinked.

Then he remembered the banquet being held in the Guildhall. Oh my God, he thought, the Prime Minister is attending.

Casually he sauntered down the street, but once round the corner, he radioed headquarters, explaining his suspicions. Could the model in the Burberry be live? He was certain of it and, if so, would be in contact with the hit man.

The Prime Minister's car was already nearing its destination. In a few minutes, it would pass the gent's outfitters. Was it already too late to foil a possible assassination plot?

A couple of minutes later, pandemonium broke loose. Police squad cars hurtled through the city streets, some blocking the path of the Prime Minister's car, while others surrounded the back and front entrance of the men's outfitters.

With barely a minute to go, the assassination plan had misfired. Fred, alias The Squirrel, had not reckoned on a constable of PC Chalmer's calibre upsetting his calculations.

Small Boy, realising the game was up, tried to make a hasty escape, but was arrested as he shinnied down a drainpipe.

The Prime Minister arrived at the banquet only five minutes late. PC Chalmers was promoted within a short space of time and The Squirrel and Small Boy were given sentences long enough to last them a lifetime.

Under the Belfry Tower

A short play for two spirits and some dream voices

FIRST SPIRIT: It is midnight in the bat-vacant, bell-sleeping, pigeon-nesting belfry tower, under a honey-coloured harvest moon, slung in space, suspended by starry chains, floating silently, gracefully, beneath an inky-black, sooty-black, badger-black ceiling. Moonbeams filter through owl-hooting, empty-nested, leaf-losing oaks, gilding grey granite angels guarding over 'Rest in peace', 'To the dear memory of' and 'Here lies' tablets.

SECOND SPIRIT: Night shrouds stained glass Sainted and Apostled windows. Night flits eerily, unseeingly, down darkened aisles, up chancel steps sentinelled by brass, eagle-gleaming, Brasso-smelling, Bible-burdened lectern. Night moves, bathed in silver moonshine, on fragrant incense-laden wings, over pews permanently polished by seats of countless generations of worshippers – some in their beds asleep, many in their forever sleep under grassy turves, stone chippings, cement slabs, jam-potted chrysanthemums and jaded geraniums.

FIRST SPIRIT: See where Mr Buryall, antique dealer and undertaker, sits on Sundays, mentally measuring prospective clients at prayers for the sick, dying and deceased.

SECOND SPIRIT: Here's where Major Marchinhaste, VC, OBE, snores away the Sunday sermon, deep in his battle dreams of days long gone. Listen! You can still hear the echoes of his dreams in the rafters.

MAJOR MARCHINHASTE, VC, OBE: It's for Johny Turk and over the top at dawn, men…

DREAM VOICE OF FIRST KILLED: All mud, mud, mud, all blood, blood, blood!

DREAM VOICE OF SECOND KILLED: I want my mum, roast beef, raspberries, rosy lips and rock cakes and…Mum, Mum, Mum…

FIRST SPIRIT: Over here! Over here! See the vestry-hanging shadowy-shaped surplices ghosting choirboy cassocks!

SECOND SPIRIT: Look! Night's tongue laps along scratched choir stalls, under hymn book-laden ledges, licking cement-like wedges of leftover gum belonging to Sam Bean, Daniel Trapp, Ronnie Wright, Dave Tyler and…

FIRST SPIRIT: Their Sunday gown-gaping pockets are always full of…

SECOND SPIRIT: Catapults, crumpled comics, crumby combs, snotty handkerchiefs, string, white mice and sticky sweets from Mrs Stuffer's sherbet-dabbing, gobstopping, Liquorice-Allsorting shop window.

FIRST SPIRIT: What's that?

DREAM VOICE OF THIRD KILLED (FAINTLY):   Mum, Mum…

SECOND SPIRIT (SOFTLY):   Come away! Come away! The moon has gone over the hill. Dawn peels Night's garments away and the bat-vacant, bell-sleeping, pigeon-nesting belfry tower is waking.

'Haste away, haste away,
It is Day, it is Day.'

Temptation

'What have you got to tell us, Jane?' a voice called to me across the room.

Flipping through a glossy magazine, I had found a page of recipes and was avidly perusing one for spiced chicken.

Alison was holding a coffee morning for the gang, most of us having formed friendships on account of the fact that our children attended the same school. Although I was an older mum, being nearly forty when my son was born, they had accepted me into their circle.

I enjoyed these mornings. Nice to relax and chat together, hear the latest gossip and discuss various topics.

'Come on, Jane, get your head out of that book. Let's hear about your experiences.'

'What experiences?' I asked, innocently.

'We're talking about relationships with the opposite sex,' someone answered. 'You know, pre-marital and extra-marital.'

I was taken aback. The younger mums were much more open about these matters, which I found rather embarrassing. I hesitated, not wanting to be thought unsophisticated or unworldly.

'Come on, Jane, don't say you haven't had any amours. After all, you married late. Surely you must have had lots of meaningful relationships before that.'

They were looking at me expectantly. Again I hesitated. Should I fob them off with a flippant answer, say that, of course, I'd had pre-marital relationships, too many to remember? But, being of a truthful nature, I saw no reason to lie.

'I don't believe she's got anything to confess!' Teresa exclaimed, disappointment tingeing her words.

'Well, no, as a matter of fact, I haven't,' I admitted, feeling inadequate.

'Good gracious!' and 'Fancy that!' were the astonished remarks flung in my direction. They looked astounded. 'You mean you've only had one partner, Jane?' one of them remarked, incredulously.

'That's right,' I answered, half reluctantly, feeling decidedly odd, a freak.

'You should get a bit of experience in, Jane,' Linda urged. 'You've been missing out. After all, time isn't exactly on your side, is it?'

'Perhaps you should have a look at this,' Helen suggested, tossing a magazine in my direction. It was a sex magazine. I had seen that sort of book in the local newsagent's, but had never bothered to look beyond the cover. However, to humour them, I pretended to glance through it, but by then they were discussing other matters and did not notice when, feeling rather disgusted, I put it down.

Over the next few weeks, I often thought back to that conversation. Had I really missed out? It had never occurred to me that sex was an important issue, though I had noticed it was certainly a recurring topic with my younger friends. As far as I was concerned, one eventually got married, shared the same bed, had children and that was that.

Arthur, my husband, was the stolid, reliable type, undemonstrative. He worked hard to provide a nice home for the children and myself. A very predictable person. I often thought how nice it would be if he did something out of character and surprised me. Even our garden reflected his personality. Lawns and flowerbeds neatly squared off – the whole effect orderly, meticulous. I longed for some curves and a patch of floral confusion.

I had asked him why he had been attracted to me. 'You're so fresh, Jane,' he had answered. 'You don't look used like some of the others.' I had been flattered. I liked that.

Was I content? I asked myself. Was there something missing? I had never asked myself these questions before that recent coffee morning.

Then, one day, a few weeks later, when cherry blossom stained the summer sky and cuckoo calls echoed from nearby woods, temptation beckoned.

Feeling restless and finding it difficult to settle to anything, I wandered into the garden just as a car turned into our drive. 'Roger!' I called, excitedly. He was Arthur's cousin. We saw quite a bit of him and his wife Madge. They were very dear friends. Roger, always full of fun, was just the tonic and diversion I needed in my present mood.

He told me he had a couple of spare days. Madge was visiting her sister and he was at a loose end.

Over coffee we chatted animatedly before, to my

surprise, he suddenly moved closer, his arms encircling my waist.

'You know I've always loved you, Jane,' he whispered.

Alarm bells began clanging in my head, but as I opened my mouth to remonstrate, the words were stifled by his passionate kisses. Of course, I ought to have pushed him away, but I was finding the situation pleasurable and exciting.

'Come on, Jane, let's go upstairs. It can't be wrong. It's all in the family, isn't it?' he coaxed.

I was curious. What, I wondered, would it be like to experience another man's caresses? My heart was racing madly. One half of me wanted to do as he asked, the other half to draw back before it was too late. But I was mesmerised so that, when he pulled me up from the couch, I followed in a daze, out into the hall and up the stairs.

At that moment, the doorbell rang, its compelling buzz breaking the spell.

'Don't answer it,' Roger hissed.

'I must. It could be the school – an accident or something,' I muttered.

A deliveryman stood on the doorstep. He handed me a large cardboard box. Thanking him, I signed a slip and closed the door.

With trembling fingers, I lifted the lid and removed some sheets of tissue paper.

The fragrant scent of lilies of the valley rose up from the box which was filled with bunch upon bunch, their pure-white bells gleaming among dark green leaves. Whoever had sent them had surely bought up the entire stock. A scrap of paper was tucked between the flowers. Smoothing it out, I read the words:

Spotted these on way to station. Their freshness reminded me of you.

Arthur

Peace on Earth

Peace on Earth, goodwill towards men,
Fighting has broken out again
And the IRA still wield the gun.

Peace on Earth, goodwill to men,
Jesus was born in Bethlehem
To save the world and set us free
From acts of war and tyranny.

But, across the globe since time began,
Fierce wars have waged
And our Planet is one great battlefield –
Rwanda, Bosnia, Afghanistan,
Russia, Indonesia and Palestine.
One could go on and on.

As one war subsides, another commences.
Has mankind lost all his senses?
Millions of innocent lives sacrificed.
When will warfare ever cease
And the Earth rejoice in prefect peace?

Will peace on Earth, goodwill to all men,
Ever echo and echo across the land,
When murder and tyranny come to an end
And missiles and guns will be totally banned?

Oh, for a world set free from war,
When peace prevails forever more!
Is it too much to ask, too much to expect?

One day I pray there will be no strife
For many catastrophes occur throughout life
And dreadful diseases assail man's body so frail
    –
There's no room for war to make things worse.

So let us all hope and fervently sing
Peace on Earth, goodwill to all men
Forever and ever and ever
Amen.

Supermarket Shopping

It's Friday and it's shopping day
In Safeway's superstore,
As armed with ice box, purse and list,
We sally forth to spend
An hour or so selecting goods
Among those scrumptious foods.

'I have to take some bottles to the bank,'
Says Hubbs. 'I'll not be long.'
So with shopping trolley ready,
I join the busy throng.

My first stop is the apples –
Hubbs prefers the Braeburns best,
But when I put them on the scale
And realise the price, I quail.
Goodness me, how huge they are.
I think I shall suggest
He munch but half a day for lunch.

Now, wherever can he be?
Just as I thought, he's
Gossiping to one of his golfing pals,
Discussing yesterday's game, no doubt.
I suppose it would be rude to shout
And get him here damn quick.

Now next I'll choose some lemons,
Mushrooms and red peppers,
Broccoli, onions, cauli, spinach and…
Ah! Here is Henry.
'Come, come,' I say. 'We really
Haven't got all day!'

But where's my list?
Oh dear! Oh dear!
I had it here just now.
I rather fear I've lost it.
Oh dearie, dearie me!

Ah! There it is, what a relief.
I see it in that cabinet
Among the fresh, minced beef.

Off we go again. 'Now put those
With our shopping, dear.'
But, absentmindedly he lobs them
In a shopper's trolley near.
'I really am,' I quickly say,
'So very, very sorry.
My husband's mind is not today
Entirely on the job.'

From shelf to shelf we trundle on
To price the tea and coffee,
But just as I select a jar of Nescafe,
Hubbs does some calculations –
'That's not a good decision, dear,
Gram for gram this is the best selection.

You know our situation
Now we are on the pension.'

I mutter through clenched teeth,
'However did I manage
When I was in complete control
Of all the weekly shopping?
I managed it quite well
And kept within the budget.'

'Ah, there you are,' a man exclaims
As panting furiously
He spies his wife debating
Over at the deli.
'I really thought I'd lost you,'
He cried excitedly.
'Ha, ha,' she chortled, 'fancy that!
You should be so lucky, ducky.'

Now husband's missing yet again,
I bet he's pricing wines.
'Come, come, my dear, it's quite high time
We joined that long, long line
Of shoppers waiting in the queue.'

But as we near a scanning till,
Ready to pay our soaring bill,
He spies a shelf of fresh cream cakes
And lingers longingly.
'No! No! they'll make you sick,' I say.
'And they're not on my list today,
Being full of high cholesterol.

Your welfare, dear, I have to guard.
Now where is our Safeway's Advantage Card?'

But as I view the contents
Of our trolley heaped so high,
I'm filled with guilty twinges,
Meditating on all the starving millions
And count myself thrice blest
As I reflect upon the gross injustice
Of our world,
Our crazy, crazy world.

Abortion

My heart already beats to the rhythm of the
joy of life.

★

OK, I've only been in this place ten weeks,
But I can feel and I know in my fragile bones
That soon I shall be plucked out
    discarded
      aborted
          my lifeblood stopped before
          my first real breath.

Never shall I feel the warmth of the sun or be hugged
close to my mother's breast.

I should arrive in May when tenuous blossoms frost
blue skies
and soft rain falls,
But I shall never know the changing seasons,
Build snowmen in the backyard, or sandcastles
on the seashore.
Never taste the fruits of life or take my chance
with the rest.

I'm normal, no defects, nothing wrong, but
Mum doesn't want me…
I could be adopted, why not?

If only I could be heard, state my case and shout,
          'PLEASE, DON'T THROW ME AWAY.'
I'm a precious person – I have a right to be born.
          But no one is listening.

Skylarks

Short years ago, you and your kind,
Unhindered, flew the countryside,
Lords of the air,
Alone, to soar and climb.

But now usurped, your warbling song
Mingles with the Concorde's drone,
And numerous birds, man-made
That rove to far-off realms
And foreign lands.

How high you soar,
Yet would you higher rise
Like Armstrong on the moon,
Swift as rockets to the skies,
Or satellites
That clutter space with artefacts
Of fume and flame,
Obedient, computerised?

Yet you sweet things, you do no harm
But lift our hearts
With your exuberant song.

And when your little day is done,
I'm sure you'll soar and sing and trill
Among the myriad angel throng,
But Concorde never will.

A Night-Time Garden

It is night-time, and stars dust a velvet sky. Dusk drapes the garden in filmy shadows and soft breezes tremble the water in the goldfish pond, gently caressing and stroking waxen water lily petals, coaxing them to slumber. Moonbeams silver the slimy trail of a wandering snail and two prickly shapes grunt and copulate beneath a rosebush.

Moths hover fitfully and fireflies flit over fragrant flowers. A lone owl hoots monotonously from an old tree stump and doves drowsily murmur inside a high dovecote. A restless sparrow twitters in the hedgerow.

The sleeping house is shuttered, dredged in moonshine and yesterday's dreams fade and shrivel. Tomorrow's dreams have yet to be born.

Fox pads silently across the lawn and snuffles in an overturned gash bin, his snout deep in a half empty carton of sweet and sour, left over from a recent Chinese takeaway.

Cat makes amorous assignations with next door's ginger tom and nightingales carol an evening hymn, their sweet notes drenching the soft night air.

The busy world is hushed and the fevered day is spent.

It is night-time and stars dust a velvet sky.

Face in the Crowd

'You don't think she's kicked the bucket, Em, do yer?'

'Well, I must say, she looks a bit odd, sorta lifeless, wouldn't yer say?'

As Em, Lil and their families had settled themselves on the beach, they had noticed the figure reclining, seemingly asleep, in a nearby deckchair. A faded, tartan rug shrouded her body. A grey scarf covered her head. Only the face, which was pale and drawn, was visible. The lips looked bloodless.

'Can't 'elp feeling sorry for 'er,' Em went on. 'Poor old thing. Expect she's one of them there elderly spinsters living in an 'ome for ladies wot's 'ard up. Comes down 'ere to pass away a few hours. Probably don't get enough ter eat. Them places don't feed 'em all that good, yer know.'

'All those 'appy faces in the crowd, Em, and there she is with a face like a death's 'ead. I'm worried abart 'er.' Lil sounded really concerned.

'I know, let's ask 'er if she'd like a cuppa,' Em suggested. 'Then we can find out if she's OK.'

'Excuse me, dear,' Em said, leaning over the motionless figure, ''ow'd yer like a nice 'ot cuppa? I put two sugars in. That all right?'

Much to their relief, the lady stirred, opening her eyes.

'How very kind you are. That's really lovely,' she answered, in a quiet, cultured voice.

'Sounds real posh, don't she? Well, at least she's alive, poor old duck. She's certainly enjoying that cuppa, ain't she?' Em remarked.

The morning, full of the usual seaside sounds, was nearly over.

The recumbent figure in the deckchair dozed again.

'Cor, look there, Lil,' Em exclaimed in a surprised voice.

As Lil followed Em's gaze, she saw that a handsome young gentleman was standing in front of the sleeping figure, who stirred as he bent down to kiss her.

'Awfully sorry it took so long, sweetheart,' they heard him say, 'but the car wasn't ready so I had to wait a while. Come along, it's time I took you to lunch.'

'Would you please return this to those kind ladies, darling,' she said, handing him the empty cup.

'My wife has recently undergone major surgery,' he explained to Em and Lil as he handed the cup back. 'We're down here for a holiday while she recuperates. It was so thoughtful of you to offer her a hot drink. Thank you very much.'

They watched, open mouthed, as he gently helped his wife from the chair. As he did so, her headscarf fell back, revealing a mass of auburn curls and, when she smiled up at him, they saw that she was not only young but quite beautiful.

It is never easy to read the story behind a face in the crowd.

Autumn Encounter

As Elizabeth sped along the country lanes in her red Mini, she noticed that the trees and bushes had lost most of their foliage, for it was late autumn. The landscape appeared gaunt and desolate. Through the bare branches of some elms, a reddened sun dipped towards the horizon.

She was looking forward to the holiday with her friends who owned a little country inn, The Hazelnut and Squirrel. The past few weeks had been very sad, as her father, whom she had been nursing for many years, had died and she was feeling rather alone in the world. Her winsome expression and large dark brown eyes gave her an elfin-like appearance. Her black, curly hair was only lightly sprinkled with grey.

Having driven for nearly three hours, she was feeling tired, but her destination was not far away, for at the next signpost she saw that Tumbleford was only a mile distant. Glancing down at the map beside her, she noted that at the next crossroads, she must take the right-hand fork and then the second lane on the right.

She was coming up to the crossroads now. She took the right-hand fork and, after passing the first right turn, came to the second almost immediately; but, after driving a short distance, she soon realised her mistake. The lane narrowed considerably, eventually becoming little more than a muddy, grassy track which terminated in a clearing bordered by a thick tangle of blackberry bushes. Mists of autumn swirled from the fields and the evening air struck cold. She must hurry and get back on the road again before darkness fell.

As she manoeuvred the car round, something moved near the blackberry bushes and began gliding towards her. It was the figure of a tall young man and, as he came closer, she saw that his face was ashen and his eyes had a faraway look. In the last dying rays of the sun, his hair shone a fiery red. From his forehead, blood dripped from a long gash. Then, to her surprise, he vanished, seeming to melt away into the shadows. An icy sensation gripped her as, accelerating hurriedly, she drove back to the road. She felt sure the fading light had played tricks with her imagination and, in the warmth of the welcome she received at The Hazelnut and Squirrel, soon forgot about the strange apparition she thought she had seen earlier.

Alone in her room that night, the reflection of her sad, pale face in the mirror reminded her of the figure she thought she had seen by the blackberry bushes.

She was very tired and soon fell asleep, but was awoken in the early hours by the sound of deep sighs. Opening her eyes, she saw a tall figure standing by her bed. It was the young man she had seen by the blackberry bushes. His face wore a terribly sad expression and was smeared with blood.

Her screams woke her friend, who rushed into the room, thinking Elizabeth must have had a nightmare. 'I'll make you a hot drink,' she said, 'and you'll soon go off to sleep again. I expect you were overtired.'

The following night, Elizabeth was woken up yet again by the same sound and knew, before she opened her eyes, that 'he' would be standing by her bed. This time she did not scream, though her heart pounded with fright.

The figure beckoned to her. Slowly, pushing back the bedclothes, she put her feet to the ground and followed him. He led her to the window and pointed to some think woods in the distance; then, with a sigh, he disappeared.

Next morning, she got up very early and, taking a knobbly stick from the hallstand, quietly let herself out by the back door and was soon driving down the grassy track she had taken by mistake two days previously.

Leaving the car, she looked around. Dawn had only just broken. The morning sky was overcast and outlines of bushes looked insubstantial, almost sinister. Long, thin branches of tall trees pointed menacingly towards her. Normally, she would have been alarmed but, at this moment, felt nothing, only aware that something, someone, was willing her to go on.

With the aid of her stick, she gradually broke through the mass of blackberry bushes. Beyond lay a thick wood, the tree trunks gnarled and ridged. Leafless branches clacked against one another in the wind like dry bones.

As she rested on a tree stump to recover from her exertions, she heard the now familiar sound of sighing. Looking round, she saw 'him' a short distance away and, like one in a dream, slowly followed where he led. Now he began to hurry and she matched her pace with his. Deep into the woods he plunged. For Elizabeth, time was nothing; exhaustion was nothing. Gradually, the trees gave way to sparse vegetation and the going was downhill.

The ground was soggy under her feet, but still the mysterious figure went on, always a few paces in front. At last, he stopped near a clump of tall reeds, but before she could catch up with him, he had vanished.

Peering through the weeds, she saw to her utter astonishment the wreckage of an aeroplane. One wing pointed crazily to the sky, the other was embedded in bog. Edging closer and treading carefully over thick, grassy tussocks, she cleared away an accumulation of mud and weeds until the cockpit was visible. Through the dirt-stained hood, the pilot's skull confronted her, staring though eyeless sockets.

Now reaction set in and she felt sheer terror. Turning away she fled back the way she had come. A strong wind blew, sighing and moaning through the branches. Footsteps sounded behind her. Twigs snapped beneath her feet. A grotesquely distorted root tripped her up and she lay among dead leaves, screaming with fright, unable to move.

Then she realised she was not alone. Leaning against a nearby tree, she saw the stranger and noticed the wings of a pilot above the pocket of his jacket. He was smiling and had lost that awful tired look. No blood dripped from his forehead. Picking herself up, she began to walk towards him but, even as she did so, he melted away into the shadows and she knew he would never return. Her fear gave way to a feeling of peace and tranquillity and she made her way back to the car without difficulty.

Back at The Hazelnut and Squirrel, everyone was very worried about her, as it was past breakfast time when she returned. After she had related her adventure, the village policeman was informed.

Headlines in the local paper stated that VISITOR HAS VISION AND FINDS LOST AIRMAN. And for some weeks, Elizabeth's story was the main talking point in the village. It appeared that the plane had crashed many years ago, during the Battle of Britain and, because the spot was so isolated, it had never been discovered.

Gradually, life settled back to normal. Elizabeth enjoyed helping in the bar and one morning was asked to unlock the door at opening time. She expected to see old Matthew waiting there. He was always their first customer but, to her surprise, it was not his wrinkled face she saw but that of a tall gentleman. His hair was a fiery red; across his forehead was a very long scar.

She must have fainted, for the next thing she knew was that she was lying on a sofa and heard the stranger explaining to her friend that he had come up from Cornwall to talk to the lady who had found the aeroplane.

'The pilot was my twin brother,' he told them.

Still feeling somewhat shaky but gradually recovering, Elizabeth asked him how he got the scar on his forehead.

'Tried to jump a breakwater years ago and missed it,' he said, ruefully.

Over lunch, he told them his name was Peter and Elizabeth told him of the visions she had experienced and how she found the aeroplane. Later, when they were alone, he asked her a lot of questions about herself, then said he owned a farm in the west country. David, his twin brother, had volunteered for the Royal Air Force when war was declared, but he, Peter, had to stay and help his father run the farm. Both he and David had been in love with Susan, the daughter of the country vet, but Peter knew it was David she loved and would eventually marry. Soon after David was reported missing, Susan told him she was expecting David's child.

'I married her a few weeks later,' Peter said, 'but soon afterwards she was killed in a riding accident.'

'Oh, how awful for you!' Elizabeth exclaimed.

'Yes, it was,' Peter answered, 'but I was kept so busy on the farm that there wasn't much time for feeling sorry for myself. My parents are dead and I'm thinking of selling the farm, but haven't yet decided where I want to live. In fact, we both seem to be at the crossroads, Elizabeth. Don't let's analyse what has happened, but I believe, in some strange way, we were meant to find each other.'

He took her hand in his and they both knew that for both of them this was a new beginning.

Missing

'Don't ask me that again, Bill, I've told you before, I absolutely refuse to chop down that tree.'

Matt shuffled across the lawn to his cottage, his old felt hat pulled well down over his silvery hair, his weather-beaten face wearing an expression of intense irritation. Damn that man, he thought, always on at me about my tree, saying it's grown too big and the roots are ruining his lawn.

He had planted the tree many years ago, soon after reporting his wife missing. She had been a pretty, neat lass when he had married her but, over the years, had become slovenly, uncaring, often leaving him for long periods, off visiting this one and that. He had suspected her morals too. There had been a bit of talk when she had eventually disappeared, it seemed for good. He had reported her missing and, although the police interviewed him, not much fuss had been made. Gone off with some fancy man was the verdict and now she was just a name on a list of missing persons.

But Matt knew old Bill suspected him of doing away with her. He thinks I buried her under that tree; he's dying to have it uprooted and confirm his suspicions, the silly old fool, Matt thought.

Time passed, then one night there was a terrible storm. Winds of hurricane force tore at the trees. Heavy rain fell relentlessly. Matt's tree was uprooted, leaving a large hole, half filled with water. Around the perimeter, several large bones protruded and a woman's slipper floated on top of the water.

There was an investigation. Old Bill saw to that, but the bones proved to be beef bones buried by Matt's Alsatian dog many years ago. The dog had obviously buried the slipper as well. That had shut old Bill up. Now the hole had been filled in and Matt would plant another tree later on.

Smiling grimly, Matt strolled down the garden path to inspect his vegetables, which, as usual, were flourishing. He thought back to the last time his wife had turned up after one of her long absences. There she was when he had returned from work, the ashtray full of cigarette ends, a gin bottle half empty on the table. He had been so disgusted that, without thinking, he had lashed out at her. She had fallen, striking her head on the iron fender. Death had been instantaneous. Well, he was not going to do time for that slut. No one would believe it was an accident so he had kept quiet.

Reaching the compost heap at the end of the garden, he prodded it with a stick. His old dad's words came back to him: 'Get a good compost heap going, lad,' he had advised. 'That's the basis of good gardening.'

Years ago, he had done just that. Dug it well down, lining the sides with bricks, and now he was reaping the rewards.

'Well, old girl,' he murmured, crumbling the loam between thumb and forefinger, 'you were useless to me living, but dead, my dear, you've proved your worth.'

Fifty-word Mini-sagas

Night Assassin

Terrified, she tensed, hearing footsteps under her bedroom window. Glass shattered. Sheer panic seized her.

Heavy breathing accompanied a measured tread as someone climbed the stairs.

The door handle clicked and, when a shaft of moonlight caught the glint of steel as the knife plunged, she surrendered to the inevitable.

Burnt Toast

Trapped in the blazing wreckage, he faced death, regretting it was too late to tell Mary he loved her. Too late to apologise about the daily bickering over burnt toast.

Waking, he realised he had been dreaming.

He sniffed.

'You stupid woman,' he screamed. 'You've burnt my bloody toast again.'

Art Form

(Seen in the Office du Tourisme,
Cognac, France)

Lovers standing naked, embracing,
She, her back pressed close against his chest,
Uplifts her arms to clasp both hands behind his
    head,
While he, circling her body,
Explores with one hand her rounded belly,
Legs interlaced,
Bronzed bodies gleaming,
Never to know fulfilment,
A sculptor's dream in wood,
Suspended in time and space –
Forever chaste.

Marigolds in March

(Rockborne, Dorset, March 1989)

Was I hallucinating
Seeing them blooming?
No! There they were blazing,
Needing no encouragement.
How dare they! How blatant!
Gate-crashing Spring,
Making the daffodil
Pale in comparison.
How shocking
To see them mocking,
Bold as brass,
Glaring defiance,
Loud, uncouth,
Shouting abuse,
Most unseemly, greedy,
Quite obscene,
Stealing the scene.
Marigolds in March
Outrageous.

The Art Exhibition

As soon as I saw it
I wanted to own it
That beautiful picture
Depicting

Cream cow suckling calf in a summertime
    meadow,
Standing knee-deep in a field full of clover
Sprayed by cream petals of may and of elder.

'How much is that picture?'
I asked the commissioner.
'Afraid it's only on loan by the owner,
Part of a private collection
Just for this special Spring Exhibition.'

I sighed, feeling sad – how I wanted that
    picture,
That beautiful picture on loan by the owner,
Part of a very private collection.

So I wrote to the owner
Who solved my dilemma,
For very soon after
I married the owner.

And now I'm joint owner of that beautiful
    picture

Depicting
Cream cow suckling calf in a field full of clover,
Part of a very private collection.

Haiku

(Japanese Poetry)

Sweet-scented lily
Shivering ecstatically
Raping bee swelling.

Cowslip in a Flowerbed

Today I found a cowslip flowering in a garden bed
                looking
                                ridiculous
                                        incongruous
                standing aloof from other blooms
                        rigid with pain
                                humiliated
                                        hanging its head
        Quite out of place, displaced – a refugee.

It isn't right to violate a cowslip in a flowerbed –
Cowslips should thrive in meadows, in scattered
                        clumps, in pastures,
                among sweet-smelling grasses.

But where are all the meadows, the grasslands and the
                        pastures?
                Alas! So many gone now
                buried under supermarkets, motorways,
                        large estates and car parks,
                sprouting DIYs and motor cars and trollies.

How I grieve for that wild flower alone in an alien clod
                among so many strangers.
                        It's pitiful,
                        pathetic
                and sad, so very sad.

Blue Rape

Flax fields rippling, breeze blown,
Gossamer seas, aquamarine, blue-green,
Slender-stalked, gracile,
Genus *Linum usitatissimum*.

Do silverfish swim in those grey-green depths
And are those dolphins leaping
From that blue hazed, quilted ocean,
splashing and plunging?

Flax flowers, dainty flowers,
Source of linseed, linens, laces,
Nature's munificence –
This wondrous manifestation,
This masterpiece of nature.

My Bulb Bowl

It only comes out once a year,
My old bulb bowl in green –
About the end of August
When I dust away the cobwebs
And fill it full of compost,
Then plant three nice fat bulbs
Of hyacinths, pink or white and
Sometimes blue.

It sits inside the gazebo
Under the staging in the dark
Where it stays for weeks in limbo;
Then, during late November,
When winter's rime paints trees,
My hyacinths there put forth their green
And ready then are they
To come into my room all bright
And very gradually
Unfurl their fragrant flowers
To perfume yuletide hours
While spring's sweet blooms
Lie still entombed in earth.

★

My goodness, how the year has flown,
It's time to plant again.

Ode to a Mole

Do you hear the Earth's heart thudding
In you subterranean dwelling?
Feel the downward thrusting root
Brush against your velvet suit?

Sightless to the skimming swallows,
Blinded by the sunlit meadows
As you scrabble, delve and burrow
Like a small elusive shadow.

Born to toil beneath the turf
      Making
           mounds
                and mounds
                    of earth.

Child of My Womb

Just for a little while longer I hold you
Safe under my heart and cushioned from
    danger,
Though you struggle and chafe in the waters
    around you.

Eager for life, you long to be free,
Free from the cord which binds you to me,
But ere the red rose its petals has shed
A pathway of pain I alone must tread.

So soon you and I must surely part
And with your going you take a piece of my
    heart.
Tomorrow I give you up to the world,
Child of my womb, my darling child.

Too Late

Have we gone too far with civilisation,
Gone over the top with modernisation and
  mechanisation,
Nuclear fission and automation?
Did our problems all start with the Industrial
  Revolution
When man left the land and began mass-
  producing?

Too long have we squandered Earth's riches
  and treasures,
Invented, invented, without thought of
  conserving
Or sensibly planning to deal with recycling
Or curbed the exploding population.

Is there any solution, any salvation
For a world where man has gone over the top
  with civilisation?
Is it all downhill, have we gone too far?
What have we done to our beautiful world?

But the writing is plain to see on the wall,
Too late, too late for civilisation,
No one listened or heeded the warning,
They only debated without taking action
And went on producing, populating, *polluting*.

Haiku

Snowdrops pierce iron earth
Brittle-headed petal heads
Braving winter frosts.

★

Foam-flecked wave, wrinkling,
Licking and lapping soft sand,
Leaving a tidemark.

★

Buttercups glowing
Fireflies flitting, fluttering
In the filmy dusk.

★

Dappled doe concealed
Crouching close in fronded fern
Sleeping in the shade.

Memories

Yesterday I saw wisteria
Hanging like tiny, purple clouds
Against an old stone wall
And I remembered:

Remembered another such day –
Was it so long ago in May?
When the world was golden with sunshine
And the cuckoo called all day
And your eyes, as blue as summer skies,
Laughed into mine.

Do you remember or have you long since
    forgot
That day in May
When wisteria hung in tiny, purple clouds
Against an old stone wall
And we kissed?

The Killing Roads

Underneath the thundering wheel
Flesh and skin and bone congeal,
Furred and feathered corpses writhe.

Left for dead or wounded lie,
Do we hear their plaintive cry?
Heedless, speeding, roaring by,
Nature's creatures born to die
Too soon.

Man has much to answer for,
Tainted and besmirched by gore,
Blood of dumb defenceless things,
Birds with broken, splintered wings,
Rabbits, ponies, foxes, weasels,
Stoats and voles, mice, otters, squirrels.
Victims of the modern world,
Splattered, strewn across the road,
Wounded hedgehog, pheasant, toad,
Killed by cruel steel machines,
Cruel as traps, inhuman, mean.

Passing by, we barely glance.
Do we wince or do we blanch
At the common circumstance
Of the mangled body there,
Injured badger, deer or hare?

Do we ever give a care?
Do we ever shed a tear?

One less creature in the wild
By the human race defiled –
Thus is man diminished.

Every Guy has His Day

Oh my goodness! What excitement there is in the woodshed this morning. If only you could pop your head round the door and take a look. They're putting me together from wood shavings stuffed into ladies' tights and an old sack. Now I'm being dressed in a pair of tattered jeans, their granddad's ancient tweed jacket and his old, mildewy felt hat. My facemask is grotesque, so they say, as, screeching with laughter, they fix it on, but when I saw my reflection later in a shop window, I thought I was a real handsome guy.

'Steady there, what's your game?' I shout. Well I never, I'm being dumped into an old truck and trundled out into the street.

'Penny for the guy! Penny for the guy!' they're chanting.

'Oh dear!' Old ladies scuttle off as I approach. Kids shriek, pointing at me, but some of the passers-by throw money into a tin box at my feet.

Now I'm wheeled up the garden path and lifted high on top of a huge pile of logs, twigs, newspapers and all kinds of rubbish. What a view! I can see the Friesian cows chewing the cud over in Farmer Tomkin's field and there goes the old black cat out mousing. I feel very important sitting up here.

It's beginning to get dark now and lots of people are crowding around my perch, all muffled up against the cold, in woolly caps, scarves and gloves.

'Stand away!' someone shouts as the bonfire is ignited. Slowly the flames take hold, devouring the paper and twigs.

Now the fun starts. Kids twist spluttering sparklers, which shoot out brilliant flashes. Catherine wheels twirl, spinning in a frenzy of crazy orbits, spewing out showers of saffron and silver sparks. Rockets zoom skywards, shedding crimson and violet blossoms lighting up the sky, which is now as black as jet.

The fire casts flickering shadows over the bystanders. Their faces appear distorted and weird as they gasp and whoop at every successive spectacle. Oh, I am enjoying myself! I'm nice and warm up here and don't mind being pelted with apple cores and conkers.

Now the fire burns furiously and, as I look down into the flames, I can see resin bubbling from the wood. The bubbles shine in the glare like drops of pearl.

Gradually, the blaze is swallowing up the logs as they spit and crackle. Smoke spirals, branches burn brittle, then subside. Leaves give off a pungent aroma and, as they scorch and curl, look like fragile brandy snaps.

A light breeze carries an odour of fried sausages and onions on its breath, sandwiched between an acrid smell of wood smoke. White-hot ash is drifting and falling like snowflakes on the damp grass.

The bonfire is dwindling and shrinking and I feel myself slipping. The heat has wrinkled my mask and charred my clothes.

As the flames engulf my body, I waver, then topple, finally merging with the white-hot ash beneath me. In my death throes I hear them yelling:

Guy, guy, stick him in the eye,
Chuck him on the bonfire and there let him die.

Everyone is cheering and, as I finally expire, I feel happy because I know I've been a real good guy.

The Apple-Dapple Lady

I remember the Apple-Dapple lady who lived in a tiny cottage in the village of Mosscombe-cum-Mitchett. She was very old, yet, as the years passed, never seemed to age further. Looking at her, one was put in mind of a September apple left on the tree over winter. Her skin was weather-beaten, her cheeks shiny pink, like little satin cushions, and under bushy brows, her small bright eyes were always full of laughter.

In winter, she wore a woolly hat shaped like an acorn, shabby brown boots and a long black cape. In summer, she dressed in long, print-flowered frocks which had seen better days and, on her head, a floppy straw hat decorated with faded, artificial poppies, which she tied under her chin with long pink ribbons.

No one could tell you her age, nor give you her proper name. If asked, she would answer with a toothy grin, 'I'm just the Apple-Dapple lady, m'dear.'

Though her cottage was small, one up, one down, her garden was large. Apple, plum and pear trees formed an archway across a winding path at the front, where two nanny goats named Dorcas and Daisy nibbled the sweet grasses and wild flowers, thus saving her the trouble of scything. They also provided her with milk; some she sold to the village folk or used for making cheese.

In summer, roses scrambled for space among the honeysuckle which ran riot over the mellow brick cottage walls. The garden at the back, behind the hawthorn hedge, blazed with colour in summer, where brilliant flowers grew in harmonious confusion, jostling with herbs and all kinds of vegetables. Here a bush of lavender, there nasturtiums cheek by jowl with cabbages and carrots; a patch of marigolds mingling with lettuce, radish and onions. Foxgloves, hollyhocks and sunflowers rampaged, unchecked. Rosemary, thyme and mint of all varieties grew in clumps between rows of potatoes and love-in-the-mist popped up wherever it could find a space.

Beehives at the bottom of the back garden supplied the old lady with honey and chickens roamed free, clucking and pecking through the flowers. Every evening, Apple-Dapple chased them into the henhouse. 'We dunna wan' that ole fox a-eating you, my beauties,' she would exclaim. But when a hen ceased laying, it would soon find its way into her cooking pot. Her chicken stews, flavoured with herbs, were unsurpassed.

All kinds of scraps went into an old pot to be mashed with corn for the hens and any other waste went on the compost heap.

On Fridays, the old lady baked crusty loaves, seedy cake and fruit buns, in the large oven of her kitchen range.

As well as selling goat's milk to the villagers, she supplied them with eggs, honey, fruit and homemade wines.

The Apple-Dapple lady was, you will realise, practically self-supporting.

Folk came to her for remedies for all kinds of ailments because she was wise in the use of herbs. 'Never meddle with they,' she warned. 'Them's be right dangerous in the wrong 'ands, dearies.'

Often, children went to her with an injured animal or bird, when she would use her skill to mend a wing or heal a cut, but if, as sometimes happened, the creature was past saving, she would despatch it painlessly. Then they would watch as, wrapping the lifeless body in a mossy shroud, she laid it in soft earth under sweet-smelling herbs. Sharing her tattered hymn book, they would sing a favourite hymn: 'There is a happy land, far, far away', or 'Loving Shepherd of thy sheep'.

Afterwards, she would dry their eyes, saying, 'Don' ye fret, m'pretty dears, the little thing be away up there a-playing o' the angels,' and send them on their way with wedges of seedy cake or hunks of bread and cheese.

Most days, the locals would see her tramping across the fields, armed with a large, dilapidated, straw basket. In summer, she gathered wild mushrooms or plucked cowslips and elderflowers to make delicious wines. Later in the year, she picked tiny strawberries, blackberries, sloes and elderberries, or would search the hedgerows for hips and haws and nuts, as well as herbs for her potions. Sometimes she dragged a small wooden truck, which she filled with wood for kindling her fire.

On Sundays, whatever the weather, Apple-Dapple went to church. She loved singing the hymns but, having no ear for timing and being a bit deaf, was always a few lines behind the rest of the congregation. This never worried her and she would carry on singing alone in her thin, quivery voice so that the parson had to wait for her to finish before continuing the service.

At the end of each day, when her work was done, she sat rocking in her chair, reading from an ancient Bible by the light of an old oil lamp, before clambering up the narrow wooden stairs to her tiny bedroom under the eaves.

Then, one day, when mists of autumn curtained woods and fields and stiff breezes snatched at leafless branches, the Apple-Dapple lady fell off the tree of life. They found her in her forever sleep, slumped in her rocking chair, a sweet smile lingering on the old, wrinkled face.

She was laid to rest in the little churchyard beside a flowering cherry, which, in spring, lays a pink petalled quilt over the mossy mound. In summer, skylarks soar and sing overhead and, when winter frosts lie brittle, snowdrops triumphantly pierce the earthy blanket which enfolds her.

'Where is the Apple-Dapple lady?' the children ask.

'She has gone to sing among the angels,' they are told.

The Ghost of Sunflower Cottage

No one told me that Sunflower Cottage was haunted. It was not mentioned by the previous occupants, the estate agent, or anyone we spoke to in the village before moving in, but we had only been in the place for a few hours when I had an uncanny feeling that, as I moved from room to room, there was something shadowing me. I not only felt this presence in the house but in the garden as well. When I spoke to my husband about it, he laughed, saying that just because the property was over three hundred years old, it did not necessarily have to possess a ghost. The strange thing was that when I felt it near me, I did not come out in goose pimples, neither did I feel the hairs rise on the back of my neck.

In fact, I was sure this ghost was benign.

I found life very full, looking after my three-year-old daughter and involving myself in various village activities, but hoped to make time later on to do some research into the history of the cottage. Perhaps I could find out about previous occupants, which might throw some light on the mystery.

One day, it so happened that I was asked to help out with the Meals on Wheels service and, in one of the homes I visited, there lived a very old lady. I became quite friendly with her, often calling in for a chat. She was only too delighted to talk about the days gone by, so, during one of my visits, I ventured to ask if she had ever heard of anything unusual in connection with our cottage, or if she knew if a tragedy had occurred there at any time.

She thought for a moment, then said that as far as she could remember, she could think of nothing sinister that had taken place there, nor had her parents or anyone in the village mentioned anything untoward occurring.

I explained that my reason for asking was because I was sure there was some sort of phenomenon in our cottage. 'A sort of presence,' I added.

She had lapsed into a reverie, then told me she would always remember old Sam, who had lived in our cottage many years ago. He had owned a beautiful Labrador, who was jet black except for the right front leg, which was covered in golden hair. Everyone loved that dog, whose name was Bess. She was a regular visitor at all the local functions; in fact, no Mothers' Meeting, flower show, parish meeting or jumble sale was complete unless Bess was there. She even accompanied Sam to church on Sundays. The dog would settle herself down by the font and guard the babies in their prams while their mums took part in the service.

She was wonderful with all the children and they adored her. 'I believe she lived to a ripe old age,' the old lady added. 'Everyone was terribly upset when she died. I think Sam buried her under the old apple tree in your garden.'

Could it be, I wondered, that my ghost was a dog. If so, then it must be Bess.

That summer, the country experienced a heatwave, which lasted for many weeks. Everywhere the ground became baked hard and cracked.

One morning, while I was hanging out some washing, my daughter suddenly gave a piercing scream. Quick as lightning, I rushed to the end of the garden, where she was playing. As I reached her, I saw, to my horror, that the ground had subsided directly in front of her, but a large black dog had its large soft jaws round her arm and was pulling her backwards away from the crater.

As I took her in my arms, I noticed that one of its front legs was covered in golden hair. When I looked more closely at the subsidence, I saw a very deep hole, which later proved to be a well that had been in use many years ago.

I looked around for the dog as I carried my daughter to the house, but it was nowhere to be seen. As the garden was surrounded by high fences, it could not have got out, but there was no sign of it. Was it Bess, I wondered, who had probably saved my daughter's life?

Later, when I told my husband about the frightening incident, saying I was sure the dog had saved our daughter's life, I knew he thought I had imagined seeing the dog.

My daughter's fourth birthday was not far off and we decided it was time she had a puppy. After making several enquiries, I heard of a market gardener living in the next village whose Labrador bitch had produced a litter. When I rang him he said he was very sorry but there was only one puppy left, a bitch, and while all the rest had been pedigrees, this remaining one had not run true to form.

Oh dear! I thought, it will be the runt of the litter, but, acting on impulse, decided to go and have a look at it, taking my daughter with me.

'She's in there,' the owner said, indicating a small conservatory leading off the kitchen. We peeped in and saw that the puppy was asleep, but must have been aware of our presence. Stretching herself lazily, she scrambled out of her basket, wagging her tail vigorously, and waddled towards us. I gasped in amazement. She was jet black except that her right front leg was covered in golden hair!

He'd even persuaded a few to be more generous and spend a few hours with him at the inn some miles away. The landlord could be relied on to keep his mouth shut for a worthwhile remuneration and his wife never suspected. Would never do for her to find out.

Good God, she was the one with all the money and her old man was loaded. Of course, he was quite fond of her, but she was an insignificant little thing, no spirit, and he'd always been a womaniser. Couldn't help it.

'If yer ain't doing anything special,' the girl said, breaking into his reverie, "ow about us going somewhere cosy, eh?'

'That suits me,' he answered. 'I know a little place where we could spend a few hours.'

The girl smiled under the floppy hat.

'Wot's yer name, eh?' she asked.

'Richard,' he lied.

He took another swift look at his companion and wished he could see her face more clearly. His hand reached out to touch her leg, sliding it up to the knee. He tried to remove the bag from her lap but, as he picked it up, she hastily retrieved it.

'Oh no, yer don't,' she shouted. 'Yer leave that alone!'

The bag had been quite heavy. He wondered about it. A frightening thought sent a prickle of apprehension down the back of his neck. Did it contain a gun? Was she planning to make trouble, perhaps demand money or, worse still, the car keys, leaving him stranded?

He found her perfume provocative. An expensive brand if he was any judge. Not the sort a tart like her would buy. Probably got it for services rendered from one of her male acquaintances. He experienced a vague sense of disquiet, but gradually shrugged off his misgivings as the car ate up the miles. Turning into a narrow lane, he drove along a secluded cart track behind a small inn and parked the car.

As he led the way across the yard, the girl followed, hugging the shadows, then waited in the dim hallway while he made the necessary arrangements with the proprietor. He returned, carrying a tray bearing a bottle of whiskey, two glasses and a plate of sandwiches.

She followed him up a flight of narrow stairs to a small bedroom, where he switched on a bedside lamp which sent out a dim red glow; then she watched as he slipped off his jacket, tossing a bulky wallet and his car keys on top of a small chest. Pouring out two whiskies, he handed one to the her.

'Come on, surely you're not going to keep that hat on all night?' he exclaimed, stretching out a hand to remove it, but she jumped up hurriedly, making for the door.

'Going to 'ave a barf,' she said.

As he began to undress he saw she had left her bag lying on the bed. Now was his chance to satisfy himself that it contained nothing sinister but, to his annoyance, just as he was about to pick it up, the door handle clicked and she returned. Snatching it up, she left the room.

Oh well, he thought, perhaps he was overreacting and, anyway, he'd look damn silly if he didn't go through with it.

Meanwhile, once in the bathroom, the girl removed the hat, pulling off the wig she was wearing, then hastily scrubbed the heavy make-up from her face and ran a comb through her short dark curls. Taking a heavy torch from her bag, she went to the landing window, tiptoeing across the passage. Looking down, she saw a young man standing beside a small van. Flicking on the torch, she gave a pre-arranged signal, which was immediately acknowledged by the figure below.

Draping a bath towel over her head, which partly concealed her face, she returned to the bedroom, where the man was already between the sheets.

'In a 'urry, are yer, Paul?' she cried, emphasising the name Paul as she pulled the towel off her head.

He shot up in bed, his face registering incredulity; his jaw dropped, his mouth sagged open, as he found himself gazing into the face of his wife. Now he realised why she had not offered him a cigarette. She knew he never smoked and that perfume was the brand she always used. He'd been caught red-handed.

'It's all over, Paul,' his wife exclaimed. 'Your luck's run out,' and, turning on her heel, she walked out of his life.

Three Wishes

Make three wishes, Mother bid
As I stirred the Christmas pud,
But later when the pud was done,
They disappeared in someone's tum.

I wished upon a star so bright,
Wished three times with all my might,
But the wind my wishes tossed afar
And they never landed on my star.

I threw three pennies in a well,
A wish for each as down they fell,
Then realised the well was dry;
For my lost wishes I did cry.

Once more I sent three wishes high
To a crescent moon in a blue-black sky,
But I was thwarted yet again
When they fell back down in a shower of rain.

No more three wishes will I make,
I'll be the master of my fate,
But pray that just once in a while
Sweet Lady Luck on me will smile.

The Bid

I saw the notice in the estate agent's window, advertising an auction to be held that afternoon. Viewing was to take place that morning at ten.

Cousin Ann, with whom I was staying for a short holiday, was working so I decided to go to the auction rooms and have a look around.

The salerooms were crammed with all manner of furniture and bric-a-brac. There was an air of decay hanging in the air and, coming in from the bright sunshine, I felt a sense of apprehension, shivering as though someone had walked over my grave. I wondered about all the people who had once owned all these things and the reasons for their being sold.

A large glass cabinet containing silverware caught my eye. Glancing casually at the glittering objects, I stared in astonishment, for there in the front of the cabinet, I saw it – my beautiful silver–framed mirror. I peered more closely at it. Could it be the very one I had sold all those years ago when I had desperately needed some extra money? It had been given me by my dear husband on our first wedding anniversary – I can still see the look of pleasure on his face as I unwrapped it. The mirror was heart-shaped, surrounded by a filigree of silver birds, fruit and flowers.

Surely there had not been others like it. I knew it was very old, for when Christopher bought it from the antique shop, he was told it was certainly more than one hundred years old. If it was the one I had sold, I could verify by looking on the back of it.

I called an official over, asking if he would kindly take it out of the cabinet, holding my breath in anticipation. Yes, there it was, the inscription Christopher had had engraved on it, which read 'Love is forever'.

Christopher had died tragically soon after he had given it to me and it had been a struggle to make ends meet. Reluctantly, I had made the painful decision to part with it and had wept for hours afterwards.

I knew I had to get it back. There was a reserve price of £500 on it. Now that my finances were more healthy, I could bid for it, going up to £1,000 if necessary.

The official replaced the mirror, relocking the cabinet, but I could not tear myself away.

'It is lovely, isn't it?' a voice behind me remarked. Turning round, I found myself looking into the most amazing pair of deep, grey eyes, flecked with blue, belonging to a very tall young man. He was dressed in pale grey. Suddenly, I had an urge to tell him about the mirror. What had come over me? Here I was talking to a complete stranger, opening up my heart to him.

'So you see,' I concluded rather breathlessly, 'why I must get it back.' To make matters worse, I began to cry.

'You must think me very foolish,' I said. 'I am so sorry,' but he just smiled, a very beautiful smile and, laying his hand on my arm, wished me luck. Then, before I could say any more, he vanished. It was almost as though he had never been there at all. I shook myself. Had I imagined him? But no, I fancied I could still feel the pressure of his hand on my arm.

That afternoon, I arrived early at the auction rooms, taking a seat in the front row. The mirror was not due to come up for some time, but already I could feel my hands becoming clammy with excitement.

At last, it was brought in. Bidding began at £500 and, besides myself, there were several other bidders – one, a large florid man with a greasy face, a dealer obviously, who seemed determined to get his hands on it.

Gradually, the price soared until only the dealer and myself were left. When it reached £1,000, I knew I had lost it, for I dared not bid higher. Sick with disappointment, I saw a horrid smirk on the face of the fat, florid dealer, but as the auctioneer raised his gavel to clinch the deal, a voice called from the back of the room, 'I bid £2,000.'

A gasp went up from everyone and the dealer looked as though he was going to explode with rage. It was obvious that he was not prepared to go that high.

Turning round and craning my neck, I realised that the bid had come from the stranger in grey I had spoken to that morning. I saw he was following a steward to the office, to settle up. In spite of my distress, I was relieved that the dealer hadn't got his greasy hands on it and felt sure it would now be in safe hands.

Having no heart to stay on, I decided to leave, but as I passed the office, a clerk handed me a slip of paper. 'The gentleman asked me to give you this,' he said.

'You can collect it now if you wish.' The slip was a receipt for the mirror. I stared at it in disbelief, gasping in amazement.

'He wants me to have it,' I stammered. 'But who is he?'

'Can't tell you that,' he answered. 'He didn't give his name. Paid in new £50 notes, then disappeared. Rum do, I thought. One minute he was standing there in front of me, the next he'd vanished, almost into thin air, you might say.'

I rushed down the corridor, through the front door and out into the car park, but there was not a soul about. I must speak to him, I told myself, and ran out into the street, looking both ways, but he was nowhere in sight. I ran back to the entrance thinking he might be in one of the other salerooms and, as I did so, I saw on the ground at my feet, a catalogue giving details of the auction. It was open at the page showing a photograph of the mirror, which had been ringed. Underneath, someone had pencilled in the words 'Love is forever'.

Annilee – A Story of Survival

This is a story about a human egg which was put into a phial in a container holding many other phials. The container was filled with a special liquid which froze the contents, pending future use. It was then stored in a steel cabinet in a vault.

Now, this particular egg was one of three taken from a patient in a unit specialising in test tube babies. Two had already been implanted, resulting in the birth of healthy boys. The third was to be used later, the mother having already decided on a name for the resulting child.

'We will call her Annilee,' she had told her husband.

However, implantation was never carried out because the mother died and so the little egg called Annilee remained for many years, shut up in a phial, buried deep in a container in a steel cabinet in a vault somewhere on the planet Urtha.

But for this particular planet, time was running out. Repeated warnings from scientists and conservation pressure groups had gone unheeded and the dreaded greenhouse syndrome had become a reality.

At first, the effects had been gradual, but all too soon, swift changes had come about and pollution of the environment was widespread. Human and animal life contracted diseases caused by the poisoned air. Offspring mutated. Vegetation blackened, withered

347

and died as temperatures rose and huge seas thundered across great tracks of land when ice caps melted. Hot winds of hurricane force fanned across the globe, causing destruction and devastation. And everywhere terrible fires raged unchecked.

Finally the planet Urtha died.

★

Now, it so happened that over the centuries, beings from another sphere, living in a far-off galaxy, had been interested observers of planet Urtha, visiting at intervals in their spacecraft. They had learned a great deal about the people, their customs and technology, but had never revealed themselves, for they found the planet becoming one of violence, where pestilence, greed, corruption, misery and poverty were widespread.

They saw the gradual diminishing of resources, coupled with the indifference of the inhabitants, and their utter inability to cope with the ever-increasing effects of pollution. It was so different from their own lovely world, which was wisely governed and controlled; where poverty was unknown and everyone so happy. They were saddened that the planet which had once been so beautiful was now dead. It seemed to them such a terrible waste that nothing on Urtha could survive.

So they called together a special assembly and it was unanimously agreed that a mission be prepared and sent to the stricken planet.

Accordingly, equipment was developed to withstand

the special problems they would encounter in making a landing on the poisoned planet and a spacecraft was finally launched.

Entering Urtha's atmosphere was hazardous, but it was eventually accomplished without disaster.

After circling the planet for some time, they came to a city standing on high ground, which had come through the holocaust partially unscathed. Nothing stirred, not even the dust which lay thick everywhere.

Putting on protective suits, they left the spacecraft and, after searching for a while, came upon a laboratory which had specialised in work on test tube babies.

Making their way to the vaults, they located the cylinders they were looking for. One was selected at random – it was that which held the phial containing the egg called Annilee.

Placing the cylinder in a receptacle specially prepared for it, they stowed it carefully in the spacecraft and set off on the long journey back to their own galaxy, soaring higher and ever higher through time and space. And as they travelled, music from the celestial spheres echoed all around them and out across the starry skies and there was great rejoicing over the whole firmament, because the egg that was Annilee, as well as all the other little eggs carried in the spacecraft, were to be given the gift of life.

★

Time rolled on and all the eggs were implanted after fertilisation. In due course, the egg called Annilee developed and the child was born.

Sounds

Of
May breezes murmuring,
Cuckoos cuck-cooing,
Bumblebees buzzing,
Crickets chirp-chirping,
Wavelets lap-lapping,

Five o'clock chiming,
Tea sets a-tinkling:

My cup runneth over.

Fading Flowers

The time has come for the fading,
The fading of the flowers of my youth.

Late autumn breathes cold breath and
Frost's icy finger shrivels and fades
The summer petals
And the loves I have known
Soon will lie cold in the ground
'Neath a mantle of snow
A mantle of earth
And the flowers will all be gone
Scattered, withered and spent,
The flowers of my youth.

For they rise and flourish
And are cut down too soon,
The flowers and loves of my youth.

An Australian Cameo

(Memories of Portland, Victoria, March/April 1992)

Out here down under it is autumn
And the sere leaves fall
As with heavy heart I take my leave,
For soon I must fly far, far away
On a great silver bird, the 'Qantas' bird,
Back to my homeland across the miles
To the place of my birth.
Must leave these wild, wide open spaces,
This vast domed sky
Where night comes down swiftly.

Strange sights I have seen while tarrying here –
Koalas so cuddly and kangaroos leaping
On the long, flat skis of their legs.
Heard magpies melodic that woke me at dawn
And cicadas' incessant whirr.
Cackling kookaburras shrieking and calling
And clamorous screeching of white cockatoos,
   yellow crested.
Seen flitting rosellas flaunting fiery red feathers
And lumbering emus in a volcanic crater.

I've been to the Gariwerds, the mighty
   mountains,

Once an Aborigine stronghold,
Where forests of gum, tousled headed,
Surge grey-green like huge seas.

I have gazed in sheer wonder at the brilliance of
   flowers
Under the sky's stark glare
Where the bottlebrush bush bristles all scarlet
And wattle of yellow wafts sweet lingering
   odour
And banksias and proteas flower like fat
   candles.

From Warrnambool to the city of Melbourne
I travelled the Great Ocean Road
Where the Southern Sea crashes, raging and
   roaring
'Gainst rugged and rocky shorelines.

Deep down in a gold mine at Sovereign Hill
I sped back in time to the days long, long gone
When diggers intrepid lusted after rich treasure
And wandered amazed through a petrified
   forest
Perched high on a cliff top
Bronzed and hard baked, turned to stone.

All of this has been wondrous, like some
   fleeting dream
Out here where they say 'G'day', 'How'd yer
   go?' and
'Good on yer, mate',
Way down under.

Though I bid farewell yet part of my heart will
   ever dwell
In this far-off land across the miles,
This mighty land down under.

Voyage in a Seashell

I found it lying on a stall
In the market place –
A pure-white shell, smooth and shiny,
And, as I put it to my ear,
The busy noises round about receded
And I was swept away on a crescendo of sound
Down, down into the depths of a bottomless
    abyss
And the sea surged as I spun round and round,
Gyrating through shoals of silverfish,
Slimy seaweed strands, strange creatures,
Sea urchins and snakes.
Then I saw the rock-strewn bed of a vast ocean
Where shell-encrusted ships lay derelict and
    dead
And blanched bones danced a mad, macabre
    measure
In swift-flowing currents,
And hermit crabs scuttled
And my hair streamed undulating in long
    golden tresses
And dolphins twisted, spinning, rotating.
But as a great grey shark dived in for the kill,
I suddenly surfaced
And the sea sounds sucked, crashing, hissing
    and swishing
As the seashell shattered,

Splintering into fragments
And I was back in the market place, a piece of
 flotsam
Washed up on the turbulent crest of life on
 land.

Haiku

Summer sky reflects
Fleecy sheep and bluebell glades
Under golden sun.

Imago

I found it there upon a twig,
A bit of withered leaf, I thought,
That Autumn left behind –
But when I put it on my palm
It seemed to twitch and tremble
And as I watched with bated breath
It split right down the middle
Then underwent a subtle change,
For, from that strangely wrinkled thing
There came a pretty crinkled wing,
First one and then another,
And as I saw them both expand,
I realised I held a piece of heaven in my hand.

Narcissi

The postman called on Christmas Eve
And in my porch did leave
A large brown box marked
'FRAGILE FLOWERS'
Sent from the Scilly Isles.

Swiftly I tore the wrapping off,
Then lifted off the lid
And, as I did, the murky day took flight
As a tide of brilliant light
Came flooding in
And grey skies turned to blue
And I heard the song of spring
Like a muted murmuring.

For the box was full of sunshine
And perfume strong and sweet
Arose from golden flowers,
Masses of narcissi
Pheasant-eyed and freshly gathered
And through the days of yuletide
Bleak winter turned to spring.

Water Lily Pond

Peace and a water lily pond
And dragonflies
Darting over still water
Sun-dappled
Under sapphire skies.

White, waxen petals, pink-tipped,
Floating on green islands
And golden fish shimmering
Tails a-flicking.

Small frogs skittering
Leaping
Over
Lily pads
Making spray splinters
And diamond droplets.

Soft breezes murmuring
Peace
And a
Water lily pond
And
Silence.

The Falling of the Leaves

October and the leaves are falling
As nature sheds her summer clothes
And unashamed stands naked,
Trembling in autumn winds,
Clacking bare limbs as the sap recedes.

Shrouds of russet red lie underfoot
Masking earth's tired breast,
For the golden days are over,
The halcyon days of summer spent, bankrupt,
Gone into cold storage, in suspended animation
And the swallows have all flown.

She was very beautiful. Her eyes were the colour of gentian flowers; her hair was flaxen.

'What name shall we give her?' the delighted husband asked his wife.

'We will call her Annilee,' she answered.

Oh Why?

Why aren't I tall,
At least five feet seven?
Why am I small,
Just five feet nothing?
It just ain't fair.

And why are my legs
So podgy and short?
How I'd like to be tall,
Like a model, not short.
It just ain't fair.

My dad, he did say
When I was much younger
That into my shoes he'd put
Lots of manure
To make me grow taller,
But he never did.

I look at those ladies
Advertising sleek dresses,
Their long legs alluring
And shapes so beguiling,
But I'm just a mess
No matter the dress.

My clothes I do get
From a couturier called Stump,
Richard Stump,
I'm really a frump,
Just a dumpy dump dump.

I do try to diet
But it's all so frustrating.
I never get thinner
Or look any taller.
I guess I must settle
For being a shorty,
A bit of a porky.

I'll soon have reached eighty,
So what if I'm weighty
And only a shorty?
It's too late to worry,
I'm just rather sorry
I'm not 32" 24" 33".
It just isn't fair.
But what do I care!

Reflection

I could hardly believe my eyes
When I gazed in my mirror today.
Was that really me reflected, staring back?
Where, I wondered, were all my yesteryears
When youth was an ever-burning flame
And the sap bubbled and overflowed
And my feet sped away as on wings
And every day was an adventure?
I thought youth was forever.
Age would never dare,
Dare to show its face.
My eyes would always brightly shine,
My cheeks glow pearly pink
And hair shine copper-rich.
Surely that was only yesterday!
But now I see reflected in my glass
A mask, the mask of age,
A stranger looking out at me
With wrinkled skin and fading eyes,
Hair silver-grey.

And I cried aloud for all
My yesterdays,
But the face in the mirror mocked my tears
And as I stared into its depths
I knew it told no lies.

Days

Days come in all different colours and sizes;
Some seem so very much longer than others,
But those that you wish never ever would end
Seem to slip through your fingers like fine
    golden sand.

Some days are cheerful, many are grey,
Others are sad and dull, others are gay,
Some spent regretting the hours that we waste
Or the rough careless word that is spoken in
    haste.

Days come in all different colours and sizes;
Some days are square, some give us surprises,
Like hearing the very first cuckoo in Spring
Or finding a bank of sweet violets blowing
    under a warm west wind.

Sometimes days sparkle, shimmer and glitter,
Exotically rich as a proud peacock's feather.
One never quite knows what each new day will
  bring,
Life's just one long round of anticipating,
  anticipating, anticipating...

Moonlight

Tonight the moon is full. Its probing fingers search every crack and cranny in the little seaside town of Sandhaven-on-Sea. It bathes the seedy two-star hotel opposite the pier, camouflaging the peeling paintwork and crumbling façade, giving it an air of enchantment. See where its rays filter through gaps in the faded curtains on the adulterous couples passionately entwined in rooms 10 and 21, who have signed the register as Jones and Robinson respectively.

Out in the bay it shimmers on the tranquil water and oily patches washed in on the tide, discharged out at sea by the SS Magpie several days ago.

It pokes inquisitive fingers through the blind of Percy Flitch, the butcher, lighting up the pork sausages at 98p a pound in the chill cabinet, which Percy will sell tomorrow at the same price, marking them 'Fresh in today'.

The moon glows over the market place on the names engraved on the war memorial and on the Armistice Day poppies which lie withered and limp, resembling blobs of dried blood.

Leaving the market place, the moonlit path leads to the parish church. The great oak door is bolted and barred, but moonbeams have stolen inside through stained glass windows, gilding the brass lectern and the great cross above the high altar. The arum lilies, lovingly arranged in a large stone urn by Miss Prunella Tweedsmuir, gleam under the moon's caress. Miss Prunella worships regularly at the altar and worships the vicar also. He, however, has the care of his elderly mother, who delights in informing Miss Prunella that longevity runs in her family, a fact already ascertained by Miss P, who has inspected the tombstones in the churchyard of the family of the vicar's mother.

This leads her to the sad conclusion that it may be many years before the old lady finally relinquishes her hold on the object of her desire.

A cloud passing over the face of the moon blankets the town, but soon disperses and the brilliance returns, latching on to a pair of long johns hanging on the washing line in the garden of Diggery Vole's cottage, which dance crazily in the frolicsome breeze. Diggery, whose dancing days are over, dreams as he snores as he twitches the hours away, dreams of the night he romped with Betty Blewitt among the bluebells and loved Lucy Larkin with a great love in Larch Wood.

A field mouse blinks in the moon's glare as it scampers through the long grass. Hurry, little mouse, for the white owl is already swooping in for the kill.

Even the chapel of rest cannot escape the moon's morbid gaze as it snoops through the shuttered windows on the newly dead. There lies old Granny Wackett, aged ninety-seven, late of Clematis Row, mother of nine, twice wed, independent to the last. A coffin close by holds the body of Lord Blatherington, aged ninety, late of Duntonlea Hall, in whose great house Granny Wackett was employed as a young girl, first as kitchen maid, then graduating, as time passed, to the position of head cook. Separated in life by the gaping chasm of class, they now lie side by side, united in death, the common leveller.

Jacob Slinger sits under a patch of moonshine in a shed adjacent to his chicken run. He has mounted a night watch, hoping to shoot the fox who stole some of his birds the previous evening. There he sits, gun propped at the ready, but unfortunately Jacob took the unwise precaution of slaking his thirst at The Slug and Lettuce before his vigil and is now sleeping off the effects and so is not aware that Reynard has already paid a visit to the henhouse and is happily trotting off over the hill, carrying two of his plump fowls.

Further down the lane, the windows of the village school wink in the bright light which licks through the corridors and streaks into one of the cloakrooms. Oh dear! Some child has left a big red lunchbox in one corner. The lid is open and bears a label which states that said box is the property of one James Dale. By the look of the empty crisp bags, sweet papers, sandwich wrappings, yoghurt cartons and orange and apple peel, it is obvious that James is extremely fond of his tummy.

A bright light shines from a window of the cottage hospital, distilling the rays of the moon. Inside, a mother sheds tears of joy as her newborn child is put into her arms.

Over in the recreation ground, the moon spotlights the nocturnal copulations of several cats, their yowling rising to a crescendo of feline fervour.

A change is taking place in the eastern sky as dawn winches up the new day and the moon's light fades and wanes, glimmering fitfully through the window of Miss Prunella Tweedsmuir's kitchen, where she prepares a flask and digestive biscuits for the vicar after the early communion service.

Old Diggery Vole is already dressed and, as he fries himself a rasher and egg, is still dreaming of the things he dreamed about all through the night.

Jacob Slinger utters terrible oaths as he realises the old fox has outwitted him and so slinks home to his cottage, his mind busily fabricating a story to appease his nagging wife, who will notice the absence of the two hens when she goes to the coop at feeding time.

A brisk breeze shivers through the poppies at the foot of the war memorial and, from many dwellings, alarm clocks chivvy sleeping residents into action.

Dawn finally purges the moon's soft radiance and she glides away to wait for day to drag herself beyond the western horizon, when her beams will once more bathe the little seaside town and her bright eyes pry into the lives of the inhabitants. But she will never tell.

The Meeting

They brought the young girl out for execution as the church clock struck five. She had refused a blindfold and stood leaning against the grey stone wall, a slim figure in a fading, poppy-flowered dress, her pretty face pale as a windflower in the pearly glow of dawn. The Germans had arrested her the previous day in retaliation for the murder of one of their officers, presumably the work of the Resistance movement. Now she was to pay the penalty.

Closing her eyes, she thought of Yves, her fiancé. If only he were here and she could see him just once more, but they had taken him months ago and there had been no word. She thought of their last meeting when he had taken her in his arms, telling her to be brave, promising that one day, when all the horror was over, they would be together always.

Opening her eyes, she saw that an armoured car had drawn up, screening her from the firing party, and the driver was engaging the officer in charge in conversation.

Gazing frantically round, she noticed to her surprise a small iron gate standing open to the right of the courtyard. Without hesitation, she fled across the yard, through the gate, into an alley, across a street, down a second alley and through the market square. She was soon clear of the village and running through a thick wood. They would be on her heels soon. Already she fancied she could hear the barking of their dogs.

Now she reached the river and, jumping in, began swimming across. As a precaution, she dived underwater, but when she reached the opposite bank, there was still no sound of her pursuers.

Hauling herself out of the water, she sped through dense foliage. Gradually the trees and bushes thinned and she was in a meadow full of spring flowers. Exhausted, she lay down on the soft grass, gasping and panting. A voice nearby startled her.

'Yvette, darling Yvette, I'm here! I've come back to you!'

Miraculously her tiredness vanished as, leaping up, she ran with outstretched arms towards her lover.

★

At that precise moment, a volley of rifle fire disturbed the pigeons roosting on the roofs of buildings surrounding the courtyard. As they circled in agitation, the early morning rays of the sun glinting on their wings, a white feather spiralled slowly down, coming to rest on the body of a young girl slumped on the cobblestones. The poppies on her dress blazed blood red.

The Double Bed

If it hadn't been for Mrs Fortescue-Smythe-Wise, I wouldn't have this problem, which began when I took her into our bedroom to see the new carpet.

'My dear,' she exclaimed, staring at the king-size bed in amazement, 'don't tell me you still sleep with your husband after all these years? Why, I insisted years ago that the colonel and I have separate rooms. After all, one doesn't want too much of all that, does one?'

'All what?' I enquired, innocently.

'You know, dear,' she explained, eyeing me archly. 'All that, well, you know...nonsense!'

I looked at our bed, at the satin coverlet, the frilly pillow cases and beribboned nightdress case. The whole set-up shrieked of 'all that nonsense'. 'Voluptuous' was the only word I could think of.

'At least insist on your own bed, m'dear,' she'd advised.

I blushed, feeling sinful, and imagined the news going round the WI market, commencing with eggs, across to knits, then cakes and veg. 'Did you know, dear, that the Fullerton Foxes still sleep together?' And by the time plants got the gossip, it would be, 'Fancy, the Fullerton Foxes sleep together in the nude!'

Of course, I'd occasionally mentioned single beds to Robert, but he'd looked so crestfallen, rather like a baby about to have its dummy confiscated.

So now I was in Sharrods furniture store, where I saw just the right thing. Twin beds, divided by a unit, linked to a plush, peach headboard. Dare I order? I mentally wrestled with the problem.

The beds seemed very isolated, unfriendly; and how could I stop Robert's snores, or his bloodcurdling bawling after reading thrillers? I'd just have to lash out at him across the intervening space with the long-handled feather duster.

The beds looked so narrow. I'd be so lonely; cold too.

Suddenly my problem vanished.

'Can I help you, Madam?' the assistant asked.

'No, thank you, not today. I'm only looking,' I answered.

The One that Got Away

If it had not been for those luscious looking mackerel glaring bright-eyed at me from the fishmonger's slab, this would never have happened, I reflected, as I sat nursing my injuries, my left foot encased in plaster, my right arm bandaged from fingers to elbow. One day, I would look back and enjoy a hearty laugh at my present predicament, but that day was yet far off.

'I'll have those two fish,' I had said to the man behind the counter, pointing to the mackerel. The scales glistened on their plump, succulent bellies and I could already sense my salivary glands going into action, anticipating the taste of that rich, scrumptious flesh. With a sprinkling of mixed herbs and a few knobs of butter, they would make a very tasty supper.

The fish was unusually large so that, after preparing them, I had to search for a suitable plate. Ah! I had it. What about the elephant plate my son had brought back from one of his holidays abroad? I only used it for special occasions, because it was so enormous. Shaped in the form of an elephant, complete with protruding tail and trunk, it was quite striking, being in a violent shade of pink, the body patterned all over in orange and yellow daisies. I was very fond of that plate, gaudy though it was.

The fish fitted perfectly on the dish but, as I was about to put it into the fridge, the telephone rang.

After a chat of about twenty minutes, I suddenly remembered the fish.

'Sorry, must dash,' I said. 'Have to put my fish in the fridge.'

Rushing to the kitchen, I inspected the mackerel.

'Oh no!' I screamed, for busily engaged in whatever a fly busily engages in, there settled on my mackerel was the largest, fattest-bellied blowfly I had ever set eyes on.

Snatching up a cloth, I flicked furiously out at the brute. Unfortunately, I flicked too hard. Off flew the blowfly, but the plate and fish took off as well, sliding across the table and landing in a heap of fish and elephant parts, on the tiled kitchen floor.

The fly buzzed round and round the kitchen in frenzied fury at being dislodged from its feast, followed by my unceasing ineffectual swipes and swots, accompanied by vociferous oaths, curses and imprecations. My blood was up. I vowed instant revenge as I followed his rapid flight out into the hall and through the lounge. Never was fox hunted more assiduously by the pack than this miserable specimen of the genus *Calliphora*.

'Tally ho! Tally ho!' I screamed through clenched teeth. 'I'll get you, you rotten swine, you filthy rotten swine.'

Ah! He was now cavorting on the window pane. Bounding across the room, I lashed out, but forgot, in my haste, to step over the leather-stuffed tortoise which we used as a footstool. I went flying, clutching as I fell at a small china cabinet, which tipped over backwards taking me with it. There followed a dreadful sound of shattering glass and fragile china.

'What happened, dear?' enquired my husband on finding me prostrate on the sofa, at the same time informing me that, as he had opened the front door, an enormous, irate blowfly had buzzed angrily past his ear and out into the garden.

Time's Chariot

Don't dream of happy days of yore
And waste those precious hours,
Now that we're growing old, so old,
Hoard up each priceless day like gold.

What matters if the dust lies thick,
Cobwebs festoon the hall?
Fill up the flask, pack up the grip
And throw away the shawl.

For soon dark shadows cast their shade,
Our life is just a span,
The roses round the door will fade,
Embrace life while we can.

So take my hand and let's explore
The beauty all around,
Before the sands of time run down
And life is ours no more.

Surprise

Something exciting happened
To me the other day
When I was going shopping
Down St James's Way,
As passing a building site in town,
A youth from high above leaned down,
Smiled and wolf whistled me.
I blushed, I grinned, in quite a spin,
I really felt quite wicked.
You see, I'm not young any more –
Tomorrow I'll be seventy-four.

Haiku

Lithe muscles rippling,
Striped torso leaping, pouncing,
Tiger teeth killing.

★

Sweetly scented rose
Tantalising handsome youth
Shedding blood-red tears.

★

Cruel web of intrigue
Luring unsuspecting victim
Spider snaring prey.

The Dangerous Skies

Many years have passed by
Since man went to the moon,
An incredible feat.
But alas, up there is now cluttered
With space stations and satellites
And rockets of all types.

There is debris galore
Rotating and whirling
From spent space machinery.

Sometimes bits fall off,
Returning to Earth
With alarming velocity
Without burning up
In the scorching heat barrier.

They said they'd burn up
Before reaching here,
But that's just not true,
For all sorts of objects,
Some small and some large,
Are speeding through space
At an astounding rate.

Many enter the oceans,
Others hit land
Exploding on impact,
Some leaking toxins.

We hear that up yonder
The spaceship called *Mir*
Suffered a miss when a large
Piece of metal passed near,
Which could have proved fatal
To the astronauts there.

There is talk of a city
Being built up in space
And rockets galore
To take earthlings up there.

Already a probe is speeding to Mars.
Could there maybe some day
Be wars on the stars?

Earth has troubles enough
From natural disasters
And violence of wars.
Do we need to meddle
And reach out so far
To the bright, shining stars?

This is just the beginning,
So what happens next?
Planet Earth needs a clean up
From pollution and evil.

But what of the skies,
The dangerous skies
Raining pieces of junk
And hunks of spent metal
That settle on Earth?

Is it progress or an insurance
'Gainst Earth's eventual demise,
Or has man gone too far
In exploring the skies?

The Grass Isn't Always Greener

Maurice Mole was tired of living like a troglodyte in long, dark, damp passages and chambers. He knew there was another more exciting world outside the meadow which was his home. The rabbit family were always chattering about their outings on the *Cowslip Special*, but his parents had forbidden him to roam beyond the thick hedgerows which surrounded their territory. 'You may think the grass is greener on the other side of the meadow, my lad, but I can assure you it isn't,' his mother would often say. But Maurice was sure she was wrong and vowed he would, one day, see all the wonders waiting to be explored in the outside world.

When springtime came he began to feel very restless. 'I shall go tomorrow,' he told himself, so the very next morning, before anyone was up, he jumped out of bed, emptied the contents of his moneybox into a purse attached to a belt which he strapped around his middle and scurried up one of the long underground corridors and out into the meadow.

'Where are you off to so early?' blackbird enquired, looking down from his song post.

'I'm going to catch the *Cowslip Special* to Sanderling Bay,' Maurice told him. 'Which direction is the station, please?'

'It's straight ahead, three meadows away,' blackbird answered, then carried on singing his morning song.

The way seemed rather long. Maurice began to tire and would have liked to sit down under a nearby blackberry bush, but heard in the distance the sound of a train. Quickening his pace, he soon came to Buttercup Halt. 'A day return to Sanderling Bay,' he said, handing some money to the man in the ticket office; he felt very grown up when the clerk called him 'sir'.

The journey was even more exciting than he had imagined. He hadn't realised there were so many different kinds of meadow – some full of vegetables, some full of sheep and lambs, while in others there were cows and horses. He thought the long-legged foals looked very elegant.

When the train went over a bridge, he looked down and saw a big, broad river. People were fishing from the banks and there were lots of boats.

'Sanderling Halt,' a porter shouted as the train slowed into a station. Maurice followed the passengers into the street and, after a few minutes' walk, there right in front of him was the sea sparkling in the bright sunshine.

There was so much to see and do that he hardly knew where to start. His little body quivered in anticipation.

First he bought a stick of bright pink candyfloss. It tasted delicious, though the floss did tend to stick to his whiskers, so he found a rock pool and washed his face.

Next, he sauntered into an amusement arcade, which was great fun; then he bought a large red balloon and two ice cream cornets, one chocolate, one strawberry flavour, which he held in either hand, licking each in turn. After that, he enjoyed a large plate of fish and chips.

He began to feel rather tired and so flopped down on the sand and was soon asleep, but when he woke up he felt very hot and uncomfortable. There seemed nowhere to go where he could cool off so he began to dig a tunnel under the sand to avoid the heat of the sun. Alas, the sand was so fine that, as he tunnelled, it fell in on top of him. The stuff got into his eyes and clung to his velvet suit so he had to give up. Then he trod on his balloon, which made a loud bang and nearly frightened him out of his velvet coat.

Just then he saw a man selling iced drinks and, feeling sure a cold drink would cool him down, felt for his purse belt, but to his horror, it was missing.

'Oh dear!' he wailed. 'It must have slipped off when I was tunnelling.' He looked around, but there was so much beach and, although he searched and searched, it was nowhere to be seen. Whatever was he going to do? He was without money and, to make matters worse, his return ticket was in his purse.

He began to feel very alone and frightened. He wished his mother was with him, and oh, how he longed for the cool tunnels of his home!

However, Maurice was a very resourceful fellow. He saw that the promenade was lined with shops and cafés, so he made his way to where he saw a large man with a florid complexion, dressed in white overalls, standing outside one of the cafés. Maurice plucked up courage and asked if he wanted help in the kitchen.

The man looked him up and down. 'Well, young sir,' he said, 'there's plenty of washing up to do. I'll pay your wages when you've cleared it all up.' And he showed Maurice into a steamy kitchen at the rear of the café.

Maurice stared in dismay. He had never seen so much dirty crockery. The working surfaces were piled high with plates, cups, saucers, glasses, pans and cutlery.

'Well, no good standing here looking at it,' Maurice told himself. He must get busy. The trouble was that waiters kept bringing in more dirty crockery so that his task seemed never ending. His hands were becoming sore. He was hot and so tired. It was like being in the middle of a dreadful nightmare.

At long last he finished. He put everything away and wiped down the work surfaces. The man was very pleased with him and, as he gave him his wages, asked if he would like to work for him until the season ended. Maurice could think of nothing worse and, with a hurried word of thanks, scampered off to catch his train.

The *Cowslip Special* was already in when he reached the station. Finding a corner, he lay back, closing his eyes against the glare. His head ached. He had a pain in his tummy, but he comforted himself with the thought that he would soon be home, soon be rolling over and over in the sweet-smelling grasses, then he would scrabble along one of the cool, dark passages under the meadow to his little chamber and curl up on his mattress of dandelion flowers.

His mother was right a usual. The grass isn't always greener on the other side of the meadow.

Joy is the Colour Red

My favourite colour is red. Red in any shape or form fills me with a wonderful feeling of joy. Surely one can't be depressed or miserable with that colour around.

Think of all the lovely red things in life. How beautiful the velvet petals of a dark red rose, the brilliance of a cheeky robin's pert breast, a flower bed ablaze with scarlet geraniums; the delight in biting into a delicious rosy apple, selecting a shiny red capsicum from a market stall and mailing letters in a chunky red letterbox; even choosing a creamy, crimson lipstick from a cosmetic counter. And what can lend wings to one's feet better than a pair of soft red leather shoes?

Floral-patterned curtains are a must in my home. Violent splashes of large fiery blooms bringing the place alive on the gloomiest day.

Christmas is the colour red – splattered everywhere – on Santa's suits, red-ribboned festive cakes, glossy holly berries, red satin bows, choirboys' crimson cassocks and shiny red wrapping paper.

When days grow short and autumn winds blow chill, red-leaved trees warm the heart and, later, when a florid winter sun transforms a frosted landscape with a pinky rose colour, the heart is filled with the joy and wonder of nature's handiwork.

What a thrill to uncork a bottle of full-bodied, home-made blackcurrant wine on a chilly day, reliving in the mind happy, sunny hours gathering summer's rich harvest.

Are there masses of scarlet poppies in the Elysium fields beyond the pearly gates? There must be.

Red is my favourite colour. Joy is the colour red.

The Voyage

I recently embarked on a voyage, but did not sail away on an ocean liner or even take a ferry across to the continent. No, this voyage was nothing of that sort. It was in fact a mini-cruise up the high street of my local town, the sole purpose being to purchase an outfit to wear at my daughter's wedding.

The day stretched ahead; lots of time in which to browse and make my choice. I had no preconceived ideas or, for that matter, any particular colour in mind, but was confident that something earth-shattering would be there for me in one of the many stores, when I would exclaim excitedly, 'That's it.'

My first port of call was a popular department store, but as I glided round the rails of dresses and suits, only one word came to mind – 'Mumsie,' I said to myself. OK, so I was a 'mumsie', but why look like one? I wanted something that would elicit gasps of admiration and comments such as, 'Oh, you do look marvellous and so young!'

In another large store, I spent some time going through possible ensembles, deciding to return later, though there was really nothing to rave over.

Perhaps a boutique would be a better choice. There were two or three a short distance along the road. As I stepped into the first one, I realised my mistake too late. Glitzy was the word for it as I glanced at the models displaying way-out gear. Strident music filled the air, which was heavy with a sickly, cloying perfume. I turned, intending to beat a hasty retreat, but a brassy looking sales lady literally pounced on me, almost dragging my reluctant body over to a clothes rail.

'Just in from London, dear,' she exclaimed, as excited as an angler who thinks he has a bite. 'All the rage, dear.' Now, if there is anything I detest it is being called 'dear' by a total stranger.

'I don't think you have anything suitable,' I mumbled, anxious to get back to the safety of the street. But she wasn't going to let me off the hook so easily.

'Now, dear, look at this – made with you in mind. It's all the rage, dear,' she repeated. The garment she held up was bright orange, studded with a sort of glitter all over the bodice, the latter cut very, very low. 'Come on, dear, try it on. You'll be surprised how well it will look on you.' With that, she almost threw me into a miniscule fitting room, jerking the flimsy curtain across with a flourish.

It was suffocatingly hot in there. I felt like a lobster in a pot of boiling water. I undressed and put the revolting garment on, then steeled myself to take a look in the mirror. 'Good God!' I shrieked. Only one word came to mind – *prostitute!* My bum stuck out like a large balloon tightly encased in the shorter-than-short skirt, while the plunging neckline revealed two generous portions of boobs. I was disgusted. Tearing if off, I dressed rapidly and, flouncing into the shop, threw the wretched garment on a rail.

'Pay here, dear, I knew you'd like it,' purred the sales lady, barely looking up from manicuring her nails. 'Latest from London, dear. All the rage.'

I rushed out into the street and into the nearest café, where I gathered myself together over a cheese scone and a cup of coffee, fumbling in my bag for my bottle of paracetamol. All ideas of finding a suitable outfit had now receded. I'd make do with the blue and white polka dot. Perhaps invest in a new hat.

Thus fortified, I sailed forth into the street, deciding to window-shop for Christmas gifts.

Finding I was at the end of the high street, I retraced my steps, when suddenly my attention was arrested by a single model in the window of a small boutique. The model was wearing an off-white suit embroidered in bottle green, red and mustard. The skirt was short, the jacket long. How would I look in that ensemble? I wondered. But she was quite tall, her legs long and slim, her body sylph-like. Would it suit me? I was doubtful.

The waxen face with the high cheekbones wore a haughty, almost derisory, expression as she looked me in the eye. I imagined her lips moving – 'You're a square, a dumpling. You could never wear this outfit and look like me.'

'Bloody cheek,' I said aloud. 'I damn well can,' I mouthed back and stepped into the shop.

A middle-aged lady rose from behind a gilt table. 'Good morning,' she said. Thank goodness she hadn't called me dear. I warmed to her.

'I'm interested in that outfit,' I explained, pointing to the model. The cat was still sneering at me.

The model, now stripped and completely nude, looked obscene, like a skinned rabbit with its mean little bum. 'You're not so great after all,' I muttered as I followed the assistant into a spacious fitting room.

I was agreeably surprised to find that the suit looked very well, but called the assistant for her views. 'I wasn't quite sure it was suitable, but I must say it really does look very nice,' she assured me. I trusted her judgment, satisfied that she was being honest. The cost made a large dent in my wallet, but I consoled myself with the thought that the mother of the bride must wear something very, very special.

Leaving the shop, I glanced at the model now attired in another gorgeous outfit. The little bitch was still smirking. I was about to poke my tongue out at her, but the sales lady was looking out of the window. Pity.

The Scream (II)

It echoed out across the valleys, rebounded from mountain top to mountain top, reverberated over the oceans, that first human scream, that first terrible human scream which came from Adam and Eve when they fell from grace and God flung them out of the Garden of Eden into a hostile environment. And the scream had barely died when Eve screamed again in childbirth as she bore Cain, then Abel. And the scream continued when Cain killed Abel and Adam and Eve screamed and cried in great distress.

But the scream never died away, for, as the planet became populated, the scream continued; early man screamed in terror when wild beasts attacked, savaging him to death and the women screamed and lamented when their young ones died from disease for which there was no cure.

And as man moved from place to place, migrating to fresh pastures, other tribes tried to take their land and made war so that yet more dreadful screams, cries and loud wailing filled the air. For man could not live in peace with his neighbours. The strong overcame the weak and so it would be throughout time.

Ships brought invaders to plunder, ravage and rape and the scream intensified and increased in volume as Christians were fed to lions in Roman arenas.

Then a great man came and taught the Ten Commandments, but for many, they went unheeded and across the world warring factions killed and maimed the population and ships of war fought over the seven seas and men screamed in agony as they perished by the cannon ball or drowned in deep oceans.

At times, there was respite and peace came for some, but always the killing and murder continued, for man, although becoming, so he thought, more civilised, now produced deadlier weapons and so terrible wars raged for years when many, in the first flush of manhood, floundered in the mud of Flanders, screaming their last on battlefields far from home and far from their loved ones; their screams mingling on the wind with the cries of the bereaved.

As one conflict ended, another began, and so it went on without end and still the scream goes on and on.

Yet another dreadful war came and death rained on armies and civilians alike and many perished in the ovens of death and many perished in the inferno that was Dresden. Again, those in the first flush of manhood burnt in their blazing ships, tanks and machines of the air and the lamentation of the people was heartrending and the screams of those in torture were horrible to hear.

But the scream that was most terrible, most blood-curdling, surely a scream to end all screams, came when death fell from the sky from the biggest, deadliest weapon the world had ever known and those screams will never die away, never ever.

Will it always be so; will the screaming go on for ever, will it never die? No, never, for it will be heard throughout the world, culminating in a crescendo of discord. Screams ingrained in the desert sand, tossed on the wild waves, forever howling across the land, because like Adam and Eve, man is discontented with his lot, unable to live in harmony and reverence all life.

As time passes, catastrophic events worldwide may well result in dire consequences for planet Earth, when the screams of the population will resound from coast to coast and, when the screaming has died away, there will be no one left to scream any more, for the devastated land will turn to dust and all the screams will be stifled under the poisoned earth.

And there will be silence for ever and ever.

The Golden Years

These are the golden years,
The very precious years
Before the final curtain
And oblivion.

The wine's still red within the cup,
The fruits of life still sweet
And scents of summer yet pervade
The senses sharp and keen.

But soon the sap no more will rise
And shades of evening steal
The dying, golden, summer's rays
As darkness falls.

So sip the wine within the cup,
Drink up and feast awhile
Before the frosts of Autumn's chill
Crumple the full-blown flowers
To die upon the briar.

These are the golden years,
The very precious years
Before the final curtain
And oblivion.

Fortune's Wheel

The wheel of fortune turns
   Of its own volition
      And you can do nothing
        To stop it spinning
          From birth to death.
             It turns you around and around,
              Flipping you up
            Then throwing you down,
          For Dame Fortune is fickle.
        Don't trust her sly smile,
      She'll keep on revolving her wheel
    All the while.
When you think you're on top
   She'll flick you right off.
      She may bring good luck
        Or you might come unstuck.
           The wheel keeps on spinning
            You'll never get off,
              Just bear it and grin
           And let the wheel spin.
         Hold on very tight,
        She could loosen your spoke
     And think it a joke,
    Then turn several cartwheels
And run you right over.
   So hang on to that wheel
     And whatever she deals

Play the best hand you can,
One day you might win
Or even break even,
But you can be sure
SHE'LL HAVE THE LAST WORD.

The Protest

I was born this morning at twelve minutes past seven
Without being consulted,
Born
Screaming
Protesting
Born into an alien environment,
which filled me with fear.

Born into a world where rivers run sluggish,
Polluted and poisoned,
Poisoned by factories
Vomiting effluent
Not biodegradable.

Born into a world where oil-slicked seas grow sicker,
Burdened by waste from nuclear power,
Where gasses drift upwards
Upsetting the atmosphere.

Born into a world where earthlings die daily,
Run down by drunk drivers,
By ignorant drivers
Exceeding the speed limit.

Born into a world where forests die hourly
And farmlands lie sterile,
Where war and starvation, disease and corruption
Are widespread.

I was born this morning at twelve minutes past seven
        Without being consulted,
But several hours later, exercising free will, I went out
        on a whimper
            Still
                    Feebly
                            Protesting;

    Cot death, *they* called it,

    ONLY I KNEW THE REASON.

Oh, To Be Young Again!

I would like to be young again
And stand on the threshold of life,
Full of vigour and vim and
Fly down the street
Or freewheel a hill
Without falling flat on my face –
Oh, how I would like to be young again!

Inside this rusting, ageing cage
A teenager rattles the bars,
Longing to break loose and leap
Into the land of yesteryear,
To dance the night away without a care.

Was Faust so wicked
To sell his soul to
Mephistopheles in exchange for
Eternal youth?
I used to think so – now, I wonder.

But, alas, the years their course
Have run and spun like a spider
This tentacled cocoon,
This cage they call old age.

But it's wrong to be greedy,
To want more, more and yet more
If one's enjoyed a good life.
But oh, how I yearn to be young again!

German Underground Hospital, Channel Islands

They built it deep – impregnable
From tons and tons of concrete;
Labour and life were cheap.

Begun by German
Engineers and pioneers
And civilian builders,
Then by a vast army of half-starved
And ragged labourers:
Moroccans, Alsatian Jews,
Frenchmen, Spaniards,
Swelled in '42 by hundreds
Of wretched Russian prisoners
Captured on the Eastern front,
Marched across Europe,
Arriving in rags,
Shod in cement bags –
Slaves.
Moving thousands of tons
Of rubble – working around the clock,
Hewing out rock,
On rations barely
Life sustaining.
Dangerous work.
Many perished, some buried
Beneath rock falls
And left to rot.

The purpose to build
An underground hospital
To cope with German casualties
Should the need arise,
Safe from bombardment,
Immune to attack
From land and air.

Now a tourist attraction – a museum
Depicting the occupation,
Dedicated to the courage
And resourcefulness of the Channel Islanders
Who endured years of Nazi rule.

But listen! Can you hear
Mute stones still echoing
The pitiful cries
And anguish
Of the oppressed,
And do crushed, bleached bones
Recoil at the sight of
Trippers lolling in the sun,
Sucking lollies and ices
At the exit?

Butterflies

When sunshine's tongue
Unlocks the bud
And bids the chrysalis unfurl
And wings of butterflies uncurl
To skim the gaudy summer flowers,

    Then fills my heart
    With joy and wonder
    To see such charm
    Upon the wing
    And my soul sings.

RIP

As we followed him to his
Resting place,
A white dove fluttered down,
Leading the way
Under an archway of blossom,
Over a carpet of fallen petals
And a gentle breeze flung
The fragile flowers in our faces,
Brushing away our tears
Like a benediction.

He was my dad,
The very best,
The gentlest of gentlemen.

The Meet

The stirrup cup it has been quaffed
And hounds are restless for the off;
They're out for blood of poor old fox.

Hunt master blows his glowing horn.
Tally Ho! Tally Ho! Tally Ho!
As way across the fields they go,
Streaming over fences, ditches,
In full cry, the hunt is on.

All those hounds and all those horses,
Huntsmen in their scarlet jackets,
Chasing dumb, defenceless foxes!

Gone to earth, the bugle sounds
As fox slips safely underground
And cowers in fear inside his lair.

The hunt re-forms and gallops off,
In *full cry* the hounds race on
And soon sniff out a second victim –
Another fox is on the run.

Hounds are barking, baying loud,
The quarry flees and for an hour
Is chased,
But soon begins to tire.

The hounds close in,
The hunting horn
Blares forth again
And signals *kill*.

Home triumphant trots the hunt
As mask and brush are held aloft.

All those hounds and all those horses,
Huntsmen in their scarlet jackets,
Chasing dumb, defenceless foxes.

And as the huntsmen wine and dine
And mouth congratulations,
Under the stars and bright moonshine
There lies a patch of red-brown rust,
All that's left of Reynard Fox,
A symbol of the huntsmen's lust.

All those hounds and all those horses,
Huntsmen in their scarlet jackets
Chasing dumb, defenceless foxes.

Octopus

However did you come to be,
Strangest creature of the sea?
Rounded belly, many tentacled,
Grabbing at crabs
With your formidable
Array of capturing devices,
Emitting ink-like fluid
To deter predators,
Moving by jet propulsion,
Amazing manner of copulation.

And you, you mother octopus,
Nurturing your precious eggs
Hanging grapelike from rock crevices,
Fanning them constantly,
Starving yourself
For six months in the process
Until they hatch…
Your reward to expire
Collapsing
On the ocean floor.

The Eternal Question

Is there anybody there
Listening
To my prayer?
Or are my words all dissipated,
Squandered
In the air?

I gaze at Christ
Crucified,
Hanging above the chancel screen,
A plaster image
Unreal
And I wonder if *He* really was,
Or is,
Or merely an incredible myth
Perpetuated down the years.

Was man by *God* created,
Or did he come to be
From centuries of
Natural progression,
The restless march
Of evolution?

One questions
But the answer is
Shrouded in mystery.

I wonder if our prayers are heard,
Or are they dissipated, lost,
Tossed into the air,
Wasted?

Prunus Subhirtella Autumnalis

When Autumn winds undress the trees
And chase the crisp, brown falling leaves
And foliage from my cherry tree
Flings to the ground its Summer gown,
A mini miracle evolves,
For, as November's frosty breath
Silvers bare twigs and naked boughs,
Sweet buds, shell-pink and white unfold
To deck my tree in fancy clothes.

Through from November until Spring
Its blossoms to the branches cling
As bonny as a bride's bouquet,
Symbol of hope and joy untold,
More precious than a hoard of gold.

Cat

Cat snoops in the gloaming
Under black-furred night,
Eyes two shining points of
Iridescent light.

Meandering through moonbeams,
Straddling ridge tiles,
Chasing velvet shadows,
Yowling to the stars.

Whiskers twitching,
Tail a'swishing,
Stalking, pouncing,
Homeward padding,
Trophy squirming,
Cat flap clunking.
End of mouse.

The Reaper Cometh
or Watch Out for Father Time

He's after me,
I know he is,
Now that my years have sped,
Cos I've seen him sneaking near my bed;
But have no fear, I know his tricks,
His wily little game.

He likes to come at night,
But I'm aware he's there
Because his scythe he clonks
Against the bedroom door,
And once it tripped him up
So I made a booing sound
And he scuttled off into the night,
For it gave him a most awful fright.

The other day in Waitrose store,
I spied him buying fish,
Observing slimy, dead-eyed flounders
Draped on the marble, ice-cold counter,
So I fled and hid behind a pillar.

But as I shopped at the cold meat section,
I saw a body on the ground
And paramedics standing round;
The reaper sure had been around.

Though on my guard I still must be,
He is, I'm sure, still after me,
But he's too busy this cold winter
Dealing with cases of influenza.

Sometimes I see him at the wheel
Of a shiny, big, black Rolls,
Searching for unsuspecting souls,
Victims of the restless roads.

Next week I'm flying to far Australia,
For to see the Great Reef Barrier –
He'll never dare to follow me
All those miles across the sea.

I think I'm safe for some long time,
Although there is no guarantee
That he still hankers after me.

One day I know my time will come
When meeting him face to face,
He'll clasp me in his cold embrace,
Then he my hand will take in his
And seal my fate with an icy kiss.

Dawn's Harbinger

It was two minutes past five to be precise
When I awoke,
Still dark
And breaking sleep's restraining cords;
The cares and worries of the hours yet to come
Drifted up through channels of my mind,
Agitating my brain,
When, cutting across the silence all around,
I heard the first few liquid notes
Of dawn's harbinger
Dripping through the air,
Like honey from a golden spoon,
Filling the garden with joyous song.
And I thought how fortunate,
No cares or worries there,
No bills to pay,
No supermarket queues,
A carefree life,
Till I remembered the ginger tom on the prowl,
The menacing magpie at breeding time
And hungry winters under frost's iron grip
And marvelled at the cheerful melody.
Then, as the music rose and fell,
I slid away on those limpid, liquid drops,
Falling into a sweet, dreamless sleep,

Awaking refreshed, ready for the day
And glancing through my window,
Glimpsed the blackbird busy tugging at a worm
  in the lawn.

Autumn Lament

(For a loved one)

I saw his silvering hair,
His misting eyes.

I saw his frail, bent form,
His faltering step.

I touched his wrinkled skin,
His cold gnarled hand,
Kissed fading lips and cheeks,
Heard labouring breath.

Then sadness placed a hand
Upon my heart
And whispered, 'It is autumn,'
And I cried.

Autumn Tapestry

Blushing apples falling,
Conkers kiss Earth's floor,
Golden gorse pods splitting,
Nature's bounteous store.

Hips wear scarlet jerkins,
Copper crown on oak,
Plums in purple robing,
Copse in flaming cloak.

Heathered slopes now misting,
Bracken brittle, brown,
Crisp breeze rustling, sighing,
Tattered flags drift down.

Petunia in the Gravel

No rain for weeks,
Lawns cracked and dry,
Blooms sickly hang
Transpire in sun.

Yet growing in the gravel drive
A purple proud petunia thrives.

How strange that in the flowerbed,
Where the earth is richly fed,
All the blooms hang
Limp or dead.

Yet growing in the gravel drive
A purple proud petunia thrives.

It seems to me that from poor soil,
Tended not with care or toil,
Something beautiful can grow
And like man born he so low
Flourishes no matter how.

Ripe Fruit

Now is the time for plucking the ripe apricots
Hanging luscious like little golden lamps
    among the leaves,
Half hidden, clinging coyly –
And you and I embrace among the fallen fruit,
Our faces glowing in the deepening dusk.

The apricots were ripe and ready for plucking
The day we first found love.

October Rape

(Hurricane, October 1987)

Early one October morning,
Great winds struck without due warning.
Right across the land they hurtled,
Birch, beech, oak and elm trees toppled.

Fifteen million trees uprooted,
Woods and parks annihilated,
Towering oaks and slender pines,
Flattened, ruined in such short time.

Skylines, landscapes quite transformed,
Never was there such a storm,
Power lines, chimneys, fences, tiles,
All blown down for miles and miles.

What a shocking sight to see
All those torn up tortured trees,
All that awful devastation
By the wild wind's violation.

All those trees should be replaced,
Not a moment must we waste,
Ash, oak, beech, chestnut and lime,
Poplar, elm and forest pine.

Trees supply the air we breathe,
Succour insects, birds and beasts,
Trees give joy, enrich the earth,
Wood for homestead and for hearth.

Teach your children to conserve
All that's precious in the world.
Plants and trees are in our trust,
Not to be despoiled by lust.

Trees have many enemies –
Man and weather and disease.
It must ever be our duty
To preserve the whole world's beauty.

Ode to Planet Earth

Earth – you ball of fire
Seething beneath our feet,
Rolling around in space
To the rhythm of the spheres,
Supporting mountains, rivers, seas,
Vegetation, trees,
Animals and humankind –
Impervious to man's attempts
To shape the universe,
But crackling, quaking, cackling
At the bad mistakes we're making,
Puking, belching, spluttering
Smoke and flame and
Larva gushing.

Are you tired of Homo sapiens,
Poking, prodding, prying
Into all your private places?
Tired of all the teeming millions –
We call it the population explosion.

Do you want to shake us off?
Are you planning an *extirpation*?
Are you about to explode
In a freakish fit?
Would you fling us into orbit,
Propel Marks and Spencer to the moon,

426

And Tesco's, tills still scanning
All the overloaded trolleys?
The White House and the Taj Mahal to Mars?

Do we exacerbate your condition
By our plundering of resources
Of oil and coal and gasses
To satisfy the masses?
Do we disturb your equilibrium?
Do you intend to disintegrate,
Dismantle your mantle and
Exterminate?

Then would you somewhere out there,
Perhaps re-form a portion
Where, for sure, some clever dick,
Escaping the confusion
Will discover in some corner
An area of water,
And improvising line and hook
Fish for haddock, cod and snook
And write on a rock
Frying tonight?

The Last Day of the World

Last night I had a dream
That today would be the last day of the world
And the beauty of the earth
Would perish in a cataclysmic stroke
Coming from whence I knew not.
And I cried for all the lovely ones,
The babes, the youths and the aged ones,
The tall, tall trees and the sweet, sweet flowers,
The pearly dawn and the sunset glow...
All would be swallowed up,
    gone,
        gone,
            into oblivion.

★

But waking, I heard the blackbird's song
And the chorus of the dawn
And sunbeams filtered through the clouds.

Then I knew it was only a dream
And I wept for joy, for the world
  was still there,
Our beautiful world, so sorely tried,
  so sorely troubled.

So cherish our world lest tomorrow
   be the last,
The very last day of the world.

Printed in the United Kingdom
by Lightning Source UK Ltd.
127683UK00001B/8/A

The Hitchhiker

The black limousine purred slowly to a stop as the girl's slender figure was silhouetted in the light of the headlamps. The window slid down at the touch of a button and a cultured voice from the dim interior asked the hitchhiker, who was wearing jeans and a short fur jacket, where she was going.

'Nearest town, man,' she replied.

Settling herself on the plush upholstery, she glanced out of the corner of her eye at the driver – a long, lean individual, a bit like a sleek greyhound, she thought. A man in his late twenties.

Extracting a packet of cigarettes and a lighter from her bag, she lit up.

'Goin' far, are yer?' she asked, peering straight ahead.

Oh God! he thought, taking in her appearance more fully. I've picked up a common little slut. That dreadful auburn frizz sticking out from under the floppy hat, the latter all but concealing her face. And that mouth, painted scarlet, looked like a great gash.

Oh well, he'd make the best of it. Been pretty fortunate with his many pickups, taking advantage of his wife's periodic visits to her family up north. Most had been nice kids on their way back to the local college, trying to save a bit on fares and some not averse to a bit of back seat petting in return for the lift.

Worlds Apart

A steak with chips he had for lunch,
For dinner two large pork chops,
But the child who lived in another world
Dined on a bowl of slops.

'Today I'll breakfast on ham and egg,'
Said the man who was well fed,
'Then for my lunch some fresh-caught trout
Washed down with a tankard or two of stout,'
But the child who lived in another world
Went hungry off to bed.

'I'm tired of fish and pork and beef,
Some turkey today I'll eat,'
Said the man as he licked his full, fat lips
And downed a glass of rich, red port,
But the child who lived in another world
Lay down unfed on a ragged bed
And cried himself to sleep.

But soon the man who was overfed
Collapsed and fell down dead
From a heart condition and indigestion
And the child who lived in another world
Closed his eyes with a sigh and slowly died
From disease and malnutrition.